The Path of the Righteous Gentile

A Practical Guide to the Seven Laws of Noah

by

Chaim Clorfene and Yakov Rogalsky

Preface to the Second Edition

It has been 26 years since *The Path of the Righteous Gentile* was first published[1] as an introduction and practical guide to the Seven Laws of Noah. Since 26 is the numerical value of Y-H-V-H, the Ineffable Four-Letter Name of God indicating that He exists in the past, present, and future simultaneously, we thought it would be fitting to begin this new edition with a brief discussion of the past, present, and future of the Noahide World.

As we explained in the text of the book,[2] the Seven Laws were given to Adam in the Garden of Eden. They were repeated to Noah after the Flood and repeated twice more by Moses, once at Marah just after Israel had crossed the Red Sea[3]

---

[1] In 1987 (the new edition was completed in 2013)

[2] Chapter One, Historical Overview.

[3] Babylonian Talmud, Sanhedrin 56b

and again at Mount Sinai, two days before the Ten Commandments were spoken by the Voice of G-d.[4]

This last repetition established the Noahide Laws as a Divine Doctrine that the people of Israel were commanded to teach to all the nations of the world. That was nearly 3500 years ago.

But just as the Noahide Doctrine is the most ancient of moral codes, so is it the newest and youngest, as it is written, "*I am the first and I am the last and besides Me there is no God (Isaiah 44:6).*"

With the destruction of the Second Temple the nations of the world lost their true connection to the Torah, as it says, *"Many people will go and say, 'Let us go up to the mountain of the Lord, to the Temple of the House of Jacob, and He will teach us of His ways and we will walk in His paths (Isaiah 2:2).'"* With the Israelites in exile, the

---

[4] Exodus 24:3; commentary of Rashi

Divine Doctrine became concealed and eventually unknown.

There had been times in ancient Israel, particularly during the days of King Solomon and the First Temple period that vast numbers of Noahides, *Gerim Toshavim* (Resident Foreigners) observed the Seven Laws and lived side by side with the Jewish people in the land of Israel. In fact, the First Temple was built with the help of 150,000 Foreign Residents[5] who had taken upon themselves the observance of the Seven Laws of Noah.[6]

The presence of Noahides in Israel continued to a lesser extent during the Second Temple period. But when that period ended[7] and the Jewish people went into exile, subject to the

---

[5] Ger Toshav in Hebrew, meaning a Gentile who has accepted upon himself the Seven Laws of Noah, is settled in the land of Israel and merits financial support.

[6] II Chronicles 2:1, commentary of the Radak (Rabbi David Kimchi, 1160-1235).

[7] Rome destroyed the Second Temple and annihilated the residents of Jerusalem in the year 70 CE.

cruel hospitality of the peoples around them, the observance of the Noahide Laws fell into a dark abyss.

The Jewish people had been instructed at Mount Sinai to teach the laws to the non-Jewish nations, but not at peril to their lives. In those exilic days, if a Jew were to tell Christians or Moslems that their knowledge of God was lacking, the response would have been an attack upon the Jewish community. So the Jew was silent in exile and the Noahide Doctrine became virtually extinct. With the exception of the Khazars during the seventh through the eleventh centuries C.E., there is hardly a word mentioned about Gentiles embracing the Jewish view of spiritual matters.

Towards the end of the 19th century, a famous French Noahide came onto the scene. His name was Aimee Palliere. Monsieur Palliere had been born a Catholic, but as a result of a deep metaphysical search he rejected the idea of a trinity and came to believe in the One God of

Israel. Eventually, he became a celebrated advocate of the Noahide Laws and an honored guest speaker at Jewish congregations in France. The fact that this one person was uniquely noteworthy shows how absent from history was the Gentile's relationship with his true spiritual heritage.

Things began to change after Israel became a sovereign state in 1948. Many of the most virulent forms of anti-Semitism in the western world relaxed for a short while, largely due to guilt and pity for what happened to the Jews during the Nazi reign of terror from 1935 through 1945, when six million Jews were tortured and murdered by a society gone insane.

In the aftermath of World War II, in the United States, England, Australia, France, South Africa and other parts of the world, Jews were allowed to live without persecution and the surrounding peoples began to take an interest in the Jewish perspective of the ways of God.

A major leap forward among Jews came when the Lubavitcher Rebbe,[8] *zy'a*, began speaking about the Seven Laws of Noah in 1980. He explained that the Seven Universal Commandments had been suppressed throughout the Diaspora because no one wanted to hear Jewish wisdom. But by 1980 things had changed. Gentiles had become tolerant of what the Jew had to say, even in matters of the soul. And it was particularly so in the United States of America.

And then the Rebbe made a startling statement. He said that every nation has a ministering angel who oversees that nation, and that the ministering angel of America had accepted teaching the Seven Laws of Noah to the people. In the wake of this revelation, the Rebbe began speaking about the Noahide Laws on a weekly basis.

---

[8] Rabbi Menachem Mendel Schneerson (1902-1994), leader of the largest unified religious organization in the world with approximately 4,000 Chabad Houses throughout the world as of the year 2013.

At the time, I looked around to find a book on the subject and purchased a copy of Rabbi Aaron Lichtenstein's *The Seven Laws of Noah*. At the time, there was nothing else I could find in the English language. Lichtenstein's book compares the structure of the commandments given to Israel with the Noahide commandments. It is a well-researched scholarly work, but had little value as a practical guide.

Seeing that I could find no basic introduction to the Noahide Laws, I considered writing one, and discussed the matter with my friend and colleague, Rabbi Yakov Rogalsky. He agreed that it would be a good idea to write such a book, a guide that both Jew and Gentile could pick up and understand the essentials of this ancient doctrine.

We concluded that one factor was necessary to undertake such an ambitious project. We needed the supervision of a world-class Torah scholar, a *talmid chacham* who understood the breadth of the Noahide Code, its sources in the Torah and the Talmud and later rabbinic writings. Rogalsky suggested that we work with Rabbi Mendel Feldman, z"l, a leading rabbi and scholar in Baltimore. The Lubavitcher Rebbe gave us his approval and blessing and agreed that Rabbi Feldman was an excellent choice to oversee the project.

After Rabbi Rogalsky and I finished the first draft of the manuscript, Rabbi Feldman asked us to bring it to him and he would go over it with us. At that meeting, Rabbi Feldman examined the entire manuscript line by line, suggesting numerous additions and changes. He asked us to come back when we had finished the re-write. About six weeks later we returned to Baltimore and once more he read through the manuscript and made a few more changes. This time Rabbi Feldman said that when we complete the revision, we did not have to come back and he would give us his endorsement.

A week later, Rogalsky called me and said that there was a problem and that maybe we should abandon the project. He had that learned Rabbi Nissan Mindel, z"l, the author of many respected books, was writing his own book about the Seven Laws of Noah. We agonized over the situation and finally decided that there was room for two new books on the subject. So we continued as before.

A few years later, after *The Path of the Righteous Gentile* had been in the stores for a while, I happened to be visiting Far Rockaway and met Rabbi Mindel at the local Young Israel synagogue. He congratulated me on the book and asked if he could have permission to consult it because he was writing a book on the Seven Laws of Noah himself. Of course, I wholeheartedly gave him permission. His book never came out. This was a defining experience for me. I took it as a general rule that when doubts creep in about a project, just go forward and trust in God.

With the manuscript of *The Path of the Righteous Gentile* completed, my wife Ariela and I fulfilled a seven year dream of making *aliyah*, moving to Israel. The unpublished manuscript was one of the prized possessions we took with us.

We settled in the Old City of Jerusalem and I started searching for a publisher. A mutual friend introduced me to Rabbi Yaakov (Yanki) Rapoport, the Rosh Yeshiva of Lev Aryeh in Jerusalem, who was one of the partners in a new publishing house called Targum Press. Rabbi Rapoport read the manuscript and was glowing about it. He wanted it, but there was a complication. Targum had a distribution arrangement with Feldheim Books. And Feldheim had to approve *The Path of the Righteous Gentile,* which might prove difficult. Feldheim was an old guard Jewish publishing house and ours was a book about something that could be thought of as radically new. To approach a time-honored Orthodox Jewish publisher like

Feldheim with an innovative book is like going into an antique shop and asking, "What's new?"

Yanki Rapoport gave the manuscript to Rabbi Yaakov Feldheim, the head of the Israel division of the publishing house. Rabbi Feldheim responded by asking, "What is this? Torah for the Gentile? Is this kosher?" Rabbi Rapoport extolled the virtues of the book from a rabbinic point of view. He said that it was well-researched and based on source material from the Talmud and the *Rambam*.[9] He also mentioned that this book could open up a new market – *Goyim*. Huge numbers of Gentiles are certain to buy this book to understand what God wants from them.

Yaakov Feldheim was unconvinced. He reluctantly agreed that he would consider it, but he had to consult with a respected rabbinic

---

[9] An acronym for Rabbi Moses ben Maimon, also known as Maimonides (1135-1204). He was a philosopher and the first great codifier of the Talmud into a systematic legal code, the Mishneh Torah, and a medical practitioner.

authority to see if it was kosher to print such a book.

A week later Feldheim called Rapoport and informed him that he was having trouble finding someone who approves of publishing the book. Yanki Rapoport mentioned that we had a written endorsement from Rabbi Mendel Feldman, a respected scholar. Feldheim felt that Rabbi Feldman was not well known enough in mainstream circles. He needed the "shoulders" of someone famous. And everyone he had consulted with so far had either doubted the value of the book or had said outright that it had no place in the religious Jewish book market. But Rabbi Feldheim promised Yanki that he had not given up yet.

Finally, Feldheim showed the manuscript to Rabbi Chaim Zimmerman, z"l, who was known to the Torah world as Chaim Zimmerman the *Gaon* (Genius). He was a famous Rosh Yeshiva, an original thinker, a brilliant scholar who was famous for the outspoken frankness with which he addressed many issues. He read parts of the manuscript and liked it.

When Feldheim asked him, "Is it kosher to publish this book?" Rabbi Zimmerman answered him, "It is not forbidden."

Feldheim asked, "That is the best you can give me?"

"What's wrong with that?" Rabbi Zimmerman asked.

"There is nothing forbidden about publishing it," he said, "So if you want to publish it, publish it."

The Path of the Righteous Gentile became Targum/Feldheim's second publication. It was one of their steadiest sellers for nearly 25 years. As the first practical guide to the Seven Laws of Noah, it has been a key factor in helping the Noahide world develop and expand.

The late eighties and early nineties were years of dynamic growth in the Orthodox Jewish world. The primary reason for this was the great number of *baalei tshuvah*,[10] children born into secular Jewish homes who had found their way back to the heritage of their grandparents and great-grandparents. Many of these late bloomers, unlike their grandparents and great-grandparents, had Gentile friends.

The Path of the Righteous Gentile had an enthusiastic readership among these newly religious Jews. They bought the book for themselves and then they bought the book for their Gentile friends to show them that Orthodox Judaism has something to offer to the non-Jew. Slowly and without fanfare, people began to realize Judaism had a universal aspect.

The great breakthrough for the Noahides came soon after *The Path of the Righteous Gentile*

---

[10] Literally, Masters of Return.

was on the market. But it was not the book that did it. It was the internet.

The world of the Noahide was a world of individuals. There have been and still are many organizations involved in the movement, but they have provided little impetus to the dynamic development of the Noahide world. Individuals and families carry the Noahide growth genome. Organizations do not. When Rabbi Mendel Feldman started becoming popular as an advisor to Noahides, he asked the Lubavitcher Rebbe for guidance in this matter. The Rebbe told him, "Stay away from the organizations."

It is not our intent to downgrade all Noahide organizations. Certainly, *batei dinim* (rabbinic courts) and *yeshivot* (learning centers) are essential and good. But there is a tendency for the organizational man to push aside genuine inquiry in favor of politics and devotion to his own rigid platform and need to earn a livelihood.

There was a problem, however, with the Noahide society of individuals. A Noahide in Chicago had no way of knowing that there was a kindred spirit in New Orleans; how much more so between Quito, Ecuador and Kolkata, India. Theirs was a world of disconnect. The internet changed all that. Social networking via the internet has removed nearly all the natural barriers between people. Noahides are now finding each other, sharing and learning with each other and marrying each other and raising families.

There are more righteous Gentiles observing the Seven Laws of Noah in the world today than there have been since the days of the First Temple.[11] Their world may be made up of individuals, but it is growing exponentially.

Ironically, it was Rabbi Chaim Zimmerman, the *Gaon*, who was the most passionate advocate of

---

[11] Jews are not keen on census-taking (see II Samuel 24:10-15) and it has been difficult to get any kind of definitive head count.

individualism in Orthodox Judaism. He taught that the individual is of infinite value, and stands on a par with the entire Jewish community. He wrote, "Society is made to serve man, but man is not made to serve society. When man starts serving society as an end, he loses his individuality and becomes subjected to the state. This is *avodah zarah* (idolatry)."

According to Rabbi Zimmerman, "The people of Israel have only one purpose, and that is to benefit the individual and improve his level of intellectual and moral excellence. In Judaism, not only is it forbidden to sacrifice a human being for society, it is also forbidden to sacrifice a human being for the sake of God, as we see in the cancellation of Abraham's sacrifice of his son, Isaac. Such sacrifice is unadulterated paganism. To the extent that Islam subordinates the individual to society or does not acknowledge the infinite worth of the individual, it conduces to the paganism exemplified by suicide bombers, whether they explode themselves in Jerusalem or in New York. Their saying "Allah is great" only makes man as well as his Creator pathetically small."

One remarkable and unexpected event concerning the Noahide Laws took place in Israel during the early 1980's. Rabbi Yosef Gerlitsky, a prominent rabbi in Tel Aviv, realizing the importance of the Seven Laws of Noah as the pathway to peace, sought to distribute leaflets about the Noahide Laws to Arab schools in Israel. He printed one hundred thousand flyers introducing the Seven Laws, but before he could distribute them to the schools, a committee of Muslim clerics in Israel stepped in and said that they would have to see the flyers and determine if these laws are acceptable to Islam. Rabbi Gerlitzky felt sure the project would be scuttled and was amazed to receive a message from the Mufti that they had accepted the leaflet and would help distribute it to the schools.

In January 2004, the current spiritual leader of the Druze[12] community in Israel, Sheikh Muwaffak Tarif, called on all non-Jews in Israel to observe the Noahide Laws as expressed in the Bible and taught in Jewish tradition. His declaration included the commitment to make "a better humane world based on the Seven Noahide Commandments and the values they represent commanded by the Creator to all mankind through Moses on Mount Sinai."

Perhaps the most surprising development has taken place in South America. In 1995, Professor Juan Mayorga translated *The Path of the Righteous Gentile* into Spanish and put online as a download. This helped stimulate interest in the Noahide Laws and today there are Noahide communities in most of the major cities throughout South America.

---

[12] The Druze are a separate ethnic group who consider Jethro, the father-in-law of Moses, whom they called Prophet Shu'aib, as their primary prophet and spiritual leader.

We are now on the brink of a new global society where Israelites and Noahides are interfacing and standing under the wings of the *Shechina*. Ancient truth is sending sparks of light into the darkness of the past 2000 years. Two peoples are emerging who define themselves by their personal relationship to God and to each other. These relationships echo the final words of the American Declaration of Independence, "And for the support of this Declaration, with a firm reliance on the protection of Divine Providence, we mutually pledge to each other our Lives, our Fortunes and our sacred Honor."

May it be God's will that this new old light becomes a moral, ethical and spiritual guide for every nation on earth. Amen.

Chaim Clorfene
Tzfat (Safed), Israel
28 Elul 5773 (5941)
September 26, 2013

Introduction

This book summarizes the Torah's call to inform and guide the Gentiles, the descendants of Noah, as to their true spiritual path in the world. Jewish readers will also be interested in learning about this little known area of Jewish study. These Seven Laws of the Children of Noah are the basic principles of civilized humanity.

For the past two thousand years, Christians and Moslems and every other religious group that has had the opportunity have been proselytizing to the Jews, telling them what their religious duty should be. The Jews, by contrast, have never actively sought converts to their own religion. Perhaps this is why few people realize that Judaism has something to say concerning the religious and ethical duties of the non-Jews in the world.

The doctrine of the Seven Noahide Commandments brings the Jewish idea of unity to the world. In fact, the very idea of unity in religion originated with Judaism. Whoever has this concept, other than the Jews, got it from the Jews.[1] And when we speak of unity, we mean both the unity of God and the unity of mankind. The unity of God means true monotheism, and the unity of mankind means a world in which all people come to God in peace and harmony.

All the religions of the world, other than Judaism, approach the idea of unity with the precept, "Believe as we believe, and the world will be one." This approach has never worked. Judaism approaches unity from an entirely different perspective. It teaches that there are two paths, not just one.[2] One path is yours. The other one is mine. You travel yours and I will travel mine, and herein will be found true unity – the

---

[1] Mishneh Torah, Laws of Idolatry, 1:2,3

[2] Ibid., Laws of Kings, 8:10

one God is found on both paths because the one God gave us both. The Noahide laws define the path that God gave to the non-Jewish peoples of the world.[3]

The Seven Noahide Commandments comprise the most ancient of all religious doctrines, for they were given to Adam, the First Man, on the day of his creation.[4] Wondrously, the Seven Noahide Commandments remain the newest and most uncharted of all religious doctrines. Humanity has managed to keep them new by ignoring them throughout history. But now, in these latter days when the footsteps of the Messiah can be heard by all who will listen closely, the Seven Noahide Commandments must finally be learned and observed by all the people of all the nations.

The word *commandment* is a translation of the Hebrew word *mitzvah*, which also means

---

[3] Ibid., 8:11

[4] Ibid., 9:1

"connection." By observing God's commandments, a person becomes connected to God's infinite will and wisdom and thereby elicits a Godly light which shines onto his or her soul. This Godly light is eternal, and in it the soul earns eternal reward.[5] By observing the Seven Noahide Commandments, a Gentile fulfills the purpose of his creation and receives a share of the eternal World to Come, the blessed spiritual world of the righteous.

The hurdle that must be cleared in preparation for observing the Seven Noahide Commandments is the acceptance of the idea that mankind's way to the Father is through the oral tradition of Judaism, known as the Oral Torah. Rebellion against the sanctity and authority of Oral Torah has been with us since those first days in the Wilderness of Sinai when the followers of Korah led a revolt against absolute authority of Moses, as we learn in the Book of Numbers, *"And*

---

[5] Likutei Torah, Rav Shneur Zalman of Liadi, Bekhukotey, page 45, column 3

they assembled themselves against Moses and against Aaron and said to them, You assume too much; for the whole of the congregation are all of them holy, and the Lord is among them; wherefore then will you lift yourselves up above the congregation of the Lord? (Numbers 6:3)."

In the end, God performed a great miracle to demonstrate His preference for the Mosaic authority, *"And the earth opened her mouth and swallowed them and their houses and all the men that were for Korah and all their wealth. And they went down, they and all who were for them, alive into the pit; and the earth closed over them and they disappeared from the midst of the congregation (Numbers 16:32,33)."*

When God gave the Torah to the Jewish people on Mount Sinai, all the people accepted the Written Torah willingly, but God had to lift the mountain over their heads and threaten to drop it on them to persuade them to accept the Oral

Torah.[6] If the Jews had difficulty in accepting the Oral Torah as no less divine than Scripture, how much more difficult must it be for the non-Jews. But accept the oral tradition[7] they must, for the source of understanding the Seven Noahide Commandments is found in the Talmud and later rabbinic teachings, and nowhere else.

There is a second difficulty that arises when considering the Seven Noahide Commandments. It is seemingly a semantic problem, but it has profound implications. The Gentile as well as the Jew should relate to members of the non-Jewish nations of the world as Noahides, a strange new term. Seen as the Children of Noah, or Noahides, the Gentile nations at once have a unique and specific

---

[6] Babylonian Talmud, Shabbat 88a. The oral tradition (primarily the Talmud and later Code of Jewish Law), according to rabbinic tradition was revealed by God to Moses at Mount Sinai, then transmitted orally from father to son, teacher to student throughout the ages. This is known as the *Mesorah* (the Heritage).

[7] The rabbis referred to are those rabbis who themselves accept the authority of the Oral Torah.

spiritual role in the world, one that is exceedingly exalted. The Children of Noah are co-religionists with the Children of Israel. Together, they are peaceful partners striving to perfect the world and thereby give God pleasure and satisfaction. By viewing himself as a Noahide, the Gentile becomes like the Jew, in that he is a member of a people whose peoplehood, not just his religion, is synonymous with its relationship to God.

At this time, *The Path of the Righteous Gentile* is the only book that presents a framework of the divine code of the Seven Noahide Commandments in a practical form, albeit a limited and seminal one. For reasons explained in the first chapter, Historical Overview, previous treatises on this subject were written by Jewish scholars for other Jewish scholars and were intended to remain theoretical and academic. *The Path of the Righteous Gentile* is a call to action for the Jew and the Gentile, the Israelite and the Noahide. And as Rabbi Tarfon said: The day is short, the task is considerable, the workers are lazy, the reward is great, and the Boss is insistent.[8]

It all depends on us, which includes you. And so, this introductory book about the Seven Laws of the Children of Noah has been prepared. It is meant not as a document of final authority, but as a means by which people may become familiar with the subject and incorporate it within their lives.

We hope and pray that the God of Abraham, Isaac, and Israel will forgive any errors this work may contain, and that it will become an instrument for bringing all mankind closer to its Father in heaven. May His revealed Presence soon dwell among us.

---

[8] Chapters of the Fathers, 2:20.

Chapter One

Historical Overview

The code of Divine Law that we now know as the Seven Commandments of the Children of Noah has been with mankind since the creation of the first man, Adam. Though man is the crown of creation, he was created last. The reason that God created man last of all the creations was to serve as a perpetual lesson, symbolic of man's choice in the world. When he is fulfilling God's will, man sits atop everything that was created before him and is truly creation's crown. But when he falls in disobedience to God, he is last and lowest of all the creatures, lower even than the gnat, which consumes throughout its life but never eliminates waste, the symbol of ultimate selfishness. Even the lowly gnat follows God's will. Man alone has the option to transgress it.[1]

---

[1] Babylonian Talmud, Sanhedrin, 38a

When God charged Adam, *"And the Lord God commanded Adam, saying: Of every tree in the garden you may surely eat. But from the tree of the knowledge of good and evil you may not eat of it, for on the day that you eat of it you shall surely die (Genesis 2:16,17),"* this single commandment contained the source of the Seven Noahide Commandments.[2] And more, Adam was charged by God with the responsibility of teaching the laws to future generations. The verse states that God commanded Adam, "saying." Although this word "saying" appears superfluous, it is a principle of the Torah that there are no superfluous words, for everything comes to teach us something. In this case, the word "saying" indicates that God not only said the commandment to Adam, but He intended that Adam say it as well. It is a principle of Biblical analysis that when a verse states, "And the Lord spoke to Moses, saying..." it means that God

---

[2] Ibid., 58b

taught Moses something and that He expected him to teach it to the Jewish people,[3] or, as in the case of the Seven Commandments of the Children of Noah, to all of mankind.

And so, Adam taught his children the Seven Universal Laws: not to worship idols, not to curse God, not to kill, not to steal, not to engage in sexual immorality, not to eat the limb of a living animal, and to establish courts of law to enforce these laws. And so mankind developed.

The clear proof that the descendants of Adam knew these laws and were expected by the Divine Judge and Father to obey them was that 1656 years later He brought the Great Flood as a punishment for mankind's failure to keep these commandments. *"And God saw the earth and, behold, it was corrupted, because all flesh had corrupted its way on the earth" (Gen. 6:12)."*

---

[3] Rashi on Leviticus 1:1, "Saying…"

The classic Biblical commentary of Rashi[4] teaches that the corruption was sexual immorality and idol worship. The very next verse reads, *"And God said to Noah, the end of all flesh has come before Me, because the earth is filled with wickedness (Genesis 6:13)."* Rashi comments that the phrase "the earth is filled with wickedness" refers to theft. So, because of sexual immorality, idol worship, and theft (three of the seven commandments which Adam was expected to teach his children, and which mankind was expected to obey), the Creator of all destroyed all, except for a remnant which included Noah, his wife, his three sons and their wives.

When the floodwaters settled and the earth had been wiped clean of its taint, humanity no longer had to fall back on Adam as the father of all mankind. Now mankind had a new father,

---

[4] Rashi is the acronym for Rabbi Solomon ben Isaac (1040-1105), author of the most important Scriptural commentary and commentary on the Talmud. Rashi explains the simply meaning of the Torah to five year old children and yet the incisiveness of his commentary challenges even the most advanced scholars.

Noah. Unlike Adam, who failed to fulfill God's commandments, Noah was *"a righteous man, pious in his generation, and Noah walked with God (Genesis 6:9)."*

And so, with a new world and a fresh start of building it in sanctity, God reaffirmed the original seven commandments that He had taught Adam. God blessed Noah and his sons and their wives and promised that He would never again destroy the world as He had done, sealing the promise for all time by striking a covenant with Noah as mankind's father as expressed in the following verses: *"And God spoke to Noah and to his sons with him, saying: As for Me, behold, I establish My covenant with you and with your seed after you (Genesis 9:8),"* and, *"And God said: This is the sign of the covenant that I am placing between me and your children and between all the living souls that are with you for all generations. My bow I am placing in the cloud and it shall be for a sign of the covenant between Me and the earth (Genesis 9:12,13)."*

The sign of the covenant was the rainbow, which would serve as a permanent symbol of Divine benevolence. It was the first time the rainbow had ever been seen in the world, although it had been created and readied for this moment at twilight after the sixth day of creation,[5] between the time Adam transgressed and the Sabbath, when God rested from all He had made. The rainbow with its seven colors reflected the beauty and sanctity of the Seven Commandments of the Children of Noah.

* * * *

When God created Adam and placed him in the Garden of Eden, this was to be the prime dwelling place of the Divine Presence. But when Adam transgressed God's commandment, the Divine Presence withdrew and left the earth in favor of the first heaven.[6] Then, with the sin of Cain and Abel, the Divine Presence withdrew

---

[5] Chapters of the Fathers 5:8

[6] Midrash Rabba, Song of Songs, 5:1.

from the first to the second heaven. Then Enosh evoked idolatrous gods, and the Divine Presence went from the second to the third heaven. From the third heaven it rose to the fourth heaven because of the Generation of the Flood.

Although Noah was righteous enough to be spared destruction and be designated the second father of mankind, despite his efforts, he failed in his attempt to effect a true rectification of Adam's sin, which was necessary to draw the Divine Presence back to the desired residence on earth. One of the first acts Noah engaged in upon leaving the Ark was the planting of a vineyard (*Genesis 9:20,21*). Most Biblical commentaries are highly critical of this action. After all, mankind had just been destroyed. To plant a vineyard so as to grow grapes and make wine seems totally inappropriate under the circumstances. But there are those who say that Noah was attempting to rectify the sin of Adam. The Talmud states that, in one opinion, the fruit of the tree of knowledge was the grape.[7] What Adam had done was drink wine in a profane manner. It had been God's intention that Adam should wait until the Sabbath, which was to come in just a few hours, and then the fruit of the tree, the grape, would be used to sanctify the Sabbath and bear witness to the fact that God had created the world in six days and rested on the seventh.[8] It is argued that Noah knew this deeper meaning of Adam's transgression, and by planting a vineyard and using the wine for sacramental purposes, he could achieve the complete rectification of the sin. But Noah failed. He became intoxicated and was discovered naked by his youngest son, Ham, who shamed him by calling Noah's other two sons, Shem and Japheth, to see their father's drunken nakedness. Rashi comments on this verse (*Genesis 9:22*) that Ham either castrated his father or had homosexual relations with him. Shem and Japheth respectfully covered their

---

[7] Babylonian Talmud, Berachot 40a

[8] Ta'amei Haminhagim, section 393

father with a garment, but the damage had been done. Noah awoke and cursed Ham and his descendants, and the Divine Presence looked down in pity (*Genesis 9:23-27*).

The Seven Commandments of the Children of Noah remained unheeded as before the Flood except for a few righteous people, notably Shem and his great-grandson Eber, who established academies of learning for the purpose of understanding and fulfilling the Noahide Laws.[9] The academies of Shem and Eber were the first schools in the world. They are mentioned many times in the Talmud, but their profound importance is largely overlooked. The fact is that Shem and Eber were great prophets of G-d.[10] And it was Shem rather than his father Noah who spread the teachings of the Seven Laws to all who would listen. Among Shem's illustrious students were Hammurabi, Job, Abraham, Isaac, and

---

[9] Rashi on Genesis 25:22 and on Genesis 28:11

[10] Pirkei d'Rebbe Eliezer 37; Rashi on Genesis 10:25.

Jacob.[11] These schools were the lone bastion of light in the encroaching darkness of the Tower of Babel.

The generation of the Tower of Babel produced brilliant scientists. Not only did they learn to master many of the world's natural forces, such as controlling the weather, but they reasoned in their scientific wisdom that the earth had no Master, or, at least if it had a Master, that they were His equal, and they built a tower to the heavens to challenge the authority of God. They scientifically concluded that, since the Flood of Noah occurred in the year 1656 after creation, this meant that every 1656 years the heavens would shake, the depths would open, and the rains would come to destroy the earth.[12] And the Bible teaches, *"And God descended to look at the city and the tower that the children of man had built*

---

[11] Actually, Shem had passed away before Jacob reached maturity, but the academy of Shem and Eber continued and Jacob studied there for fourteen years before he journeyed to Haran to find a wife.

[12] Ibid., Genesis 11:1

(Genesis 11:5)." God's descending to look was from the fifth heaven.

God took measures to stop His errant children by confounding their language and scattering them to distant lands (*Genesis 11:4*).

Originally, all of mankind spoke one language, the holy language of Scripture, Hebrew, the twenty-two letters of the Hebrew *alef-bet* being the very instruments of creation.[13] But now mankind had lost this merit and was forced to communicate with each other in the seventy basic languages of the world.

During these times, King Nimrod arose with a wickedness that was virtually without precedent. He proclaimed himself god of all the earth and commanded all his subjects to worship

---

[13] Jerusalem Talmud, Megillah, 1:9; Rashi on Genesis 11:1

him as the actual deity. Those who refused, he killed.[14]

Nimrod was called *"a mighty hunter before the Lord" (Genesis 10:9)*." Rashi comments that the phrase "a mighty hunter" means that he captured the minds of men with his mouth and led them astray to rebel against God. "Before the Lord," Rashi says, indicates that Nimrod intentionally provoked God in His Presence. Nimrod, unlike any man who had lived before him, acted wickedly in order to defy God. He knew his Master and rebelled out of spite against Him.

God withdrew His Divine Presence to the sixth heaven in response to the sins of Sodom and Gemorrah, primarily theft and sexual perversion. In those societies, cruelty was admired and

---

[14] Zohar, p. 73; Yalkut Me'am Loez (Torah Anthology), Genesis, vol. 1, p. 356

human kindness harshly punished, often by death.[15]

The ancient Egyptians completed the job of driving God away by being wholly devoted to their many idols, more steeped in sexual perversion than the Sodomites, and by developing another form of evil to its ultimate – witchcraft.[16] With God's revealed Presence removed to the seventh and highest heaven, mankind dwelt in a world of moral and spiritual darkness.

Finally, there arose a righteous man whose deeds began to draw the revealed Presence back to earth. Abraham stood against the darkness of the world by clinging to the Creator and doing His will. He challenged Nimrod's

---

[15] Rashi on Genesis 18:21 mentions that the citizens of Sodom punished a girl with a strange and cruel death because she had given food to a poor man.

[16] Rashi on Exodus 7:22 states that when the first of the Ten Plagues (turning the Nile into blood) was accomplished, Pharaoh said to Moses and Aaron, "Do you bring witchcraft to Egypt, which is full of witchcraft?"

idolatry with his belief in the One God, and eventually vanquished Nimrod completely, bringing mankind to the recognition of God and His way in the world. In Abraham's merit, the Divine Presence descended from the seventh heaven to the sixth heaven. Because of Abraham's son, Isaac, the Divine Presence descended from the sixth to the fifth heaven, then from the fifth to the fourth through Isaac's son, Jacob.

Jacob's spiritual might was awesome. He wrestled with an angel of God and defeated it (Genesis 32:25-30). Through Jacob and his children, twelve sons and a daughter, a new and distinct people on earth emerged. The Children of Israel were named after their father Jacob, who had been blessed by God and given the new name: "*Your name shall no more be called Jacob, but Israel shall be your name, and He called his name, Israel" (Genesis 35:10).*" Rashi comments that the name Jacob implies one who comes with stealth and guile, but the name Israel denotes a prince and a ruler.

With the Children of Israel, a people of God had come into the world. Abraham, Isaac, and Israel were mighty prophets and knew prophetically that their descendants would go down to Egypt in exile and would then be redeemed by God and given His Divine Law on Mount Sinai.

The Patriarchs observed the Seven Commandments of the Children of Noah. Through their gift of prophecy coupled with the tradition they received from Shem and Eber, who were also prophets, they saw what the Sinai Revelation would bring, and observed those laws as well, even though they had not been commanded concerning them.

When God blessed Isaac, it was "*because Abraham listened to My voice, and kept My charge, My commandments, My statutes, and My laws (Genesis 26:5).*" Rashi states that the word "charge" refers to the precepts of the Torah which had not yet been commanded, including Sabbath observances, whereas "commandments" refers to matters such as robbery and murder, two of the Seven Noahide Commandments.[17]

In fact, there were times when a conflict over the Mosaic and Noahide codes of law arose. The initial strife between Joseph and his brothers had to do with the difference between the Mosaic precept of keeping the dietary laws and the Noahide Commandment forbidding the eating of the limb of a living animal. Mosaic Law permits Israelites to eat the meat of an animal that has been ritually slaughtered, even if the animal still exhibits movement in its limbs. Noahide Law does not require ritual slaughtering, but forbids Noahides to eat an animal's meat unless every trace of movement has stopped. The brothers had a heated discussion about the subject, and the sons of Leah argued that they, by following the Mosaic precept, were exempt from the Noahide prohibition. To prove the point, they slaughtered

---

[17] Rashi on Genesis 26:5

an animal according to the Mosaic precept and ate of its meat before the animal's limbs had stopped twitching. Joseph felt that they had erred in their judgment and told the matter to their father.[18] Joseph's brothers then sold him into slavery, but God was with him and he rose to become second in command in Egypt, a veritable king alongside Pharaoh. By the time he had forgiven his brothers for what they had done to him, the Divine Presence had descended from the fourth to the third heaven through the merit of Jacob's third son, Levi, who established the Jewish priesthood.

Before the Children of Israel settled in the land of Egypt, Judah, one of the brothers, preceded them and set up a house of study in Goshen so the sons of Jacob could be immersed in learning the seven Noahide commandments as well as the laws of the Torah, which they received as a heritage from Shem and Eber, and Abraham,

---

[18] Ibid., Genesis 37:2

Isaac, and Israel.[19] Even during the long and bitter period of Egyptian slavery, the priestly tribe of Levi remained in the house of study, exempt from harsh servitude, so that the Divine Law would be remembered and understood and fulfilled.[20] In the merit of Levi's son, Kohath, whose sons were destined to carry the Holy Ark of God through the Wilderness, the Divine Presence descended from the third to the second heaven.

When Pharaoh decreed death for the male infants born to the Children of Israel, Amram, the leader of the generation and another descendant of Levi, divorced his wife, Jochebed. His purpose was to stop bringing Israelite infants into the world in order to prevent their murder. Amram, as leader, knew that his action would be emulated by his people, which is precisely what happened. But his daughter, Miriam, pointed out that whereas Pharaoh had decreed only against males,

---

[19] Ibid., Genesis 46:28

[20] Ibid., Exodus 5:4

Amram had decreed against all infants, male and female, by bringing none into the world. Respecting the wisdom of their daughter's words, Amram and Jochebed remarried, and the child Moses was born.[21] In Amram's merit, the Divine Presence descended from the second to the first heaven.

Moses was the most humble man who ever lived (*Numbers 12:3*). His humility was so profound that he considered himself as nothing at all. Whatever he achieved, he saw as coming solely from God, believing that if God had blessed another man with as many talents as he, the other man would surely have achieved more with them.[22] This self-nullification stood him in stark contrast to the egomania of Pharaoh, who claimed to be a deity as Nimrod had.[23]

---

[21] Ibid., Exodus 2:1

[22] Likutei Sichot, the Lubavitcher Rebbe, vol. 13, page 30

[23] Rashi on Exodus 7:15

When God redeemed the Children of Israel and decimated the idolatry of the Egyptians, it was for the purpose of His Revelation at Sinai and the Giving of the Torah. Fifty days after the Children of Israel had left Egypt, Moses ascended Mount Sinai, and in full view of 600,000 Jewish men and at least 1,400,000 women and children,[24] the Lord God of Israel descended to earth from His heavenly abode[25] and said *"I am the Lord your God who brought you out of the land of Egypt, out of the house of bondage (Exodus 24:10)."*

God had departed from the Garden of Eden and now, twenty-seven generations later, returned on Mount Sinai and spoke all the words of the Ten Commandments. It was a Divine Revelation that is incomprehensible to the human mind. All the blind and the lame and the deaf

---

[24] Beit Elokim, Moshe of Trani, Shaar HaYesodot, chap. 47

[25] Remaining ten handbreadths above the ground.

were miraculously healed.[26] All the righteous souls who would ever be born into this world were called forth by the Lord God to witness His Divine Presence.[27] This was the seal of God, His truth.

With the Giving of the Torah, the God of Israel chose the descendants of Abraham, Isaac, and Jacob as His Chosen People, instructing them to fulfill the 613 Commandments of the Torah. He also commanded the righteous of the other nations of the world to keep the Seven Commandments of the Children of Noah and commanded Moses and his people to teach them.[28] It was both the establishment of a new covenant and the reinforcement of the old one.

The Mosaic and Noahide Laws were inextricably bound together. The Children of Noah, the righteous Gentiles, were obligated to fulfill the Seven Commandments, not because

---

[26] Rashi on Exodus 20:15

[27] The Book of our Heritage, vol. 3, p. 86

[28] Mishneh Torah, Laws of Kings, 8:11

they were given to Noah after the Great Flood, but because they were given on Mount Sinai. And it became the obligation of the Children of Israel to teach the true faith in God to the righteous Gentiles by introducing them to Seven Universal Commandments by which all nations can live in peace and harmony.

When Moses ascended Mount Sinai to meet God, earth and heaven came together in a unique way. God took of His holiness and brought it to earth. For the first time in creation, physical objects could be infused with actual holiness. The Torah scroll and other writings, the sacrifices and other articles of use in the Tabernacle and Temple service, and the Children of Israel themselves became holy unto the Lord, meaning separate and distinct from the rest of creation with a sanctity uniquely reserved for the service of God (Exodus 19:6).[29] This was the beginning of the true universal religion in which Israel, the Jewish

---

[29] Torah Ohr, Rav Shneur Zalman of Liadi, p. 68

people, is the priest and the Children of Noah, the righteous Gentiles, its faithful congregation.[30] The year was 2448 of the creation.[31]

During the periods when the Jewish people lived in the Holy Land, their responsibility for teaching the Gentiles the Seven Commandments was generally fulfilled. During the 410 years that the First Temple stood and the 420 years of the Second Temple, Gentiles who wanted to dwell in the Land of Israel agreed to fulfill the Noahide Laws and had the right to enter the Holy Temple and offer sacrifices to God (Zechariah 14:17-18).[32]

With respect to the nations of the world, this posed something of a problem. Influential as it was, particularly during the times of King

---

[30] The Unknown Sanctuary: A Pilgrimage from Rome to Israel, pp. 147-149

[31] Seder Hadorot, vol. 1, p. 83

[32] Babylonian Talmud, Sukkah 52b

Solomon, the Land of Israel was but one place on a rather large globe. And the observance of the Noahide Laws outside of the Land of Israel was rare. Then, in the year 4800 of creation, nearly two thousand years ago, God took a drastic step to remedy the situation. He destroyed His Holy Temple, the center of religious Jewish life, and exiled His people Israel to every corner of the planet, where many remain to this very day. As the Talmud states, *"The Jewish people went into exile only in order to make converts, meaning to teach the nations faith in the One God."*[33]

The intention was for the Jewish people to proclaim the faith in the God of their fathers and to bring all the peoples of the world into a spiritual union with God and Israel by teaching them the Seven Commandments of Noah. But what the Jews found in the world outside their own land was a difficult situation. Mixed up with a myriad of foreign cultures, the Jews had a lifelong

---

[33] Ibid., Pesachim 87b

struggle to maintain their own traditions without being swallowed up by the cultures and traditions of the peoples around them, in fulfillment of the Biblical injunction, *"Take heed to yourself that you inquire not after their gods, saying: How did these nations serve their gods? Even so, I will do likewise" (Deuteronomy 12:30)."* Moreover, the Jew found that people were distrustful of him and hostile, and were far too busy trying to convert him to their religions to have any time to listen to what he might have to say about the subject.

Three factors in recent times have caused a change in the situation. First, the spiritual deterioration of mankind has reached a desperate stage. Half the world follows an official doctrine of atheism (which Jews consider the cruelest and most extreme form of idolatry), and much of the rest of the world is sunk into immorality and crime. Second, there exists a new spirit of ecumenism, largely due to the internet and radio and television. These have given birth to an information explosion in which Judaism's view concerning the Gentile's relationship to God no longer meets with irrational responses.

The third factor is that God has finally brought the appointed time, as it says, "*Thus says the Lord of Hosts: In those days it shall come to pass, that ten men of all the languages of the nations shall take hold of the corner of the garment of him who is a Jew, saying, 'We will go with you, for we have heard that God is with you (Zechariah 8:23).*'"

Chapter Two

Knowing God

PART ONE – *Concerning the First Existence, the God of the Universe, God's Oneness and the negation of attributing physicality to Him.*

1. It is the foundation of foundations of all doctrines and philosophical inquiry to know that there is a First Existence without a beginning and that He created all existence from absolute nothingness. Everything that is found in the heavens or on the earth exists only because of the truth of His Existence.[1]

2. If all the creatures in creation should cease to exist, He alone would still exist and in no way would He be nullified because of their nullification. Every creation needs Him, but He, Blessed Be He, does not need any of them or all of

---

[1] Mishneh Torah, Foundations of Torah, 1:1

them, and His truth is not like the truth of any one of them.[2]

Their existence is not imperative, but depends on His existence. Therefore, their existence is relative. But the First Existence is uncaused. His existence is absolute.

3. Of Him the prophet says, "*The Lord God is truth (Jeremiah 10:10).*" He alone is truth and there is no other truth like unto His truth.[3] Of Him the Torah says, *"There is nothing else besides Him (Deuteronomy 4:35)."*

4. This Existence is the God of the universe and Master of the earth. He directs the planet with a power that has neither limit nor end, with a power that is uninterrupted, so that the planet always revolves. And it is impossible for something to revolve without there being a force causing it to

---

[2] Ibid., 1:3

[3] Ibid., 1:4

revolve. He, Blessed Be He, causes it to revolve without a hand and without a body.[4]

5. And if it should ever occur to you that there is another deity besides Him, it is a rejection of the very Source on which everything depends.[5]

6. This God is one. He is not two or more than two, and there is no single existence that is unique and singular like His existence. He is not in a category that includes others of His species. And He is not divided into portions or sections as is a body. His oneness is the ultimate of simplicity and His uniqueness has no equal in the universe.[6]

7. If there were many gods, they would necessarily have bodies, because there is no way to differentiate one being from another except by bodily or material differences. And if the Creator had a body or any material form, He would have

---

[4] Ibid., 1:5

[5] Ibid., 1:6

[6] Ibid., 1:7

both a limit and an end, and His power would have a limit and an end, because it is not possible for there to be a body that has no termination point and everything pertaining to a body also has a termination point. But because of our God, Blessed Be His Name, Whose power is endless and uninterrupted, the planet revolves perpetually, for His power is not a bodily power. Because He has no body, there are no accidents or occurrences of the body that happen to Him which might divide or separate Him from another being. Therefore, it is impossible for Him to be anything but One.[7]

8. If a person should think that there might be two deities, equally uncreated, what would distinguish one from the other except for their occupying different places at the same time or the same place at different times? And if you want to say that they occupy different places at the same time or the same place at different times, they are

---

[7] Ibid.

surely not limitless. Otherwise, the concept of two infinities arises, which is by definition impossible. Infinity is one and all inclusive and supremely indivisible into aspects, extremities, or forms.

9. It is explained in the Torah and the Prophets that the Holy One, Blessed Be He, has no body, for it says, *"Because the Lord He is God in Heaven above and on the earth below (Deuteronomy 4:39),"* and a body cannot be in two places, and it says, *"Because you saw no form on the day the Lord spoke to you (Deuteronomy 4:15),"* and it says, *"And who is compared or equal to Me? (Isaiah 40:25),"* and if He had a body, He would have some basis of comparison to other bodies.[8]

10. If so, why does it say in the Torah, *"And under His feet...(Exodus 24:10),"* and *"Written by the finger of God, (Exodus 31:18),"* *"the hand of the Lord (Exodus 9:3),"* *"the eyes of the Lord (Genesis 38:7),"* *"the ears of the Lord (Numbers 11:1),"* and

---

[8] Ibid., 1:8

many examples like this? All of this is because the intellect of man is unable to fathom anything other than physicality, and the Torah is given in the language of man. So all of these examples are descriptive phrases, such as, *"If I whet the glitter of My sword, (Deuteronomy 32:41)."* Does He have a sword? It is all only a metaphor. The truth is that He has no semblance or form, but all of it is the vision revealed to the prophet, as it is written, *"Can you find God by searching for Him, or can you delve into the depths of the Almighty?" (Job 11:7)."*[9]

11. And what was it that Moses sought when he asked God, *"Please, show me Your glory (Exodus 33:18)"*? Moses wished to know the truth of the existence of the Holy One, Blessed Be He, to the point where he knew it in his heart, just as one knows a person whose form is engraved in his heart, and whom he recognizes as distinct from other men. Thus did Moses yearn to know the

---

[9] Ibid., 1:9

Holy One, Blessed Be He, to the point where He would be distinct in Moses' heart like other existences, thereby knowing the truth of God's existence as it really is. And God answered him that man, while his soul is attached to a body, lacks this power of intellect and so he cannot know this truth clearly.[10]

12. Since, as it has been explained, God has no body, He is not subject to the accidents of the body. He has neither attachment nor separation, neither place nor measurement, neither ascent nor descent, neither right nor left, neither front nor back, neither standing nor sitting, and just as He has no ending, neither has He a beginning, and He has neither life nor death as a body has, neither intellect nor wisdom like a wise man, and He neither sleeps nor wakes, and he has neither anger nor laughter, neither joy nor sadness,

---

[10] Ibid., 1:10

neither silence nor speech like the speech of man.[11]

13. And such passages in the Torah as *"He sits in the heavens and laughs (Psalms 2:4)"* are merely metaphors and similes, for as the sages of Israel teach, the Torah was given in the language of man. And God says, *"I am the Lord, I do not change (Malachi 3:6)."* If He were at times angry and at times joyous, this would surely constitute change, for all these qualities and attributes are found only in a physical body, a vessel whose foundation is dust. But He, may He be blessed, is exalted far, far above any of this.[12]

PART TWO – *Concerning the obligation to love and fear God.*

1. One should strive to love and fear God, Who is honored and exalted, as it says, *"You should love*

---

[11] Ibid., 1:11
[12] Ibid., 1:12

the Lord your God (Deuteronomy 6:5)," and *"You should fear the Lord your God (Deuteronomy 6:13)."*

2. What is the way to love Him and fear Him? When a man ponders deeply about His wondrous deeds and His manifold great creations, he will realize that God's wisdom has no equal or end, and he will immediately love and praise and glorify and desire with a great desire to know His Great Name.[13] And when he thinks about these things, he will immediately be awestruck with fear, and he will realize that he is but a tiny creature, low and inconsequential,[14] standing with extremely limited knowledge before the One Who possesses knowledge that is perfect and complete.[15]

---

[13] According to the mystical teachings of the Torah, the Name of God means the Revelation of His Divine Presence.

[14] Any being in comparison to the entire universe, and all the more so in comparison to the One who created the universe, can be considered truly inconsequential.

[15] Mishneh Torah, Foundations of the Torah, 2:2

PART THREE – *Concerning God's creation of the universe through His speaking and the continued existence of the universe through God's life force.*

1. *"Know this day and take it unto your heart that the Lord is God in the heavens above and on the earth below, there is no other (Deuteronomy 4:39)."*

2. In the beginning, when God said, *"Let there be a firmament in the midst of the waters (Genesis 1:6),"* the words of His blessed speech, being eternal as He is eternal, stand eternally in the firmament of the heavens as the activating life force in creation. Were God to retract His words or cause His speech to depart even for an instant, the heavens would immediately return to absolute nothingness just as they were prior to their having been created by God's saying, *"Let there be a firmament."*[16]

---

[16] Tanya, Gate of Unity and Faith, chap. 1, p. 76b

3. Thus it is with each of the Ten Utterances by which God created the world. Were God's speech to return to its Source, the entirety of creation would instantly cease to exist and would become the absolute nothingness that it was before the beginning of the six days of creation.[17]

4. One who contemplates the foregoing can begin to understand how God was one and unique and alone before He created the world, and remains equally one and unique and alone even after He created the world, and that the creation of the world in no way added anything to His completeness and perfection.[18]

5. This seems to be a paradox. How can it be that the creation of the world added nothing or effected no change in God? The seeming paradox is resolved by realizing that compared with God, Whose speech is the sole life force in creation, the

---

[17] Ibid. It must be understood, however, that God's speech is never separated from Him as it is with created beings, for there is no place outside of Him.

[18] Ibid., chap. 7, pp. 82b-83a

world is absolutely and literally nothing and nonexistent. This is because in His Presence everything is considered nonexistent, literally null and void, and there is no place devoid of His Presence,[19] as it is written, *"Do I not fill heaven and earth? saith the Lord (Jeremiah 23:24)."*

6. When a flesh and blood person speaks, the words and the breath of his mouth are felt and seen to leave the speaker and to become things unto themselves, but God's speech is never separated from Him, because there is no place devoid of Him and nothing outside of Him, for He is eternal and infinite.[20]

7. Even the idea of speech as applied to God is to be taken not literally but metaphorically. Just as the speech of a person reveals what was hidden in the person's thoughts, thus it is with the Lord of Hosts, Blessed Be He, Who brought forth all of created existence from a state of concealment to

---

[19] Ibid., chap. 3, p. 78a

[20] Tanya, chap. 21, p. 26b

revelation by the Ten Sayings of creation as recorded in the Book of Genesis. It is this which is called speech in reference to God.[21]

8. These Ten Sayings by which the world was created are called the speech of God because through them His will went from a concealed state to a revealed state. But this so-called speech is unified with Him in absolute unity. The difference is only from the perspective of created beings, who receive their life force from God's speech, as it descends from His exalted being and creates material existence, descending level after level until it reaches this base physical world. Here, created beings are able to receive the Divine flow of life without losing their identities and being absorbed and nullified in their true Source, God.[22]

9. This Divine influx is concealed to avoid a revelation of God that is greater than the world can endure. Therefore, it appears to the creatures

---

[21] Ibid., chap. 21, p. 26b

[22] Ibid., p.27a

that the light and life force of the Omnipresent which is clothed in each creation, and is the true existence of each creation, is a thing apart from His Blessed Self and merely issues from Him, just as the speech of a human being issues from the person. Yet there is absolutely no concealment from the perspective of the Holy One, Blessed Be He. Nothing is obscured from Him whatsoever. To Him darkness and light are exactly the same, as it is written, *"Even the darkness conceals nothing from You, but the night shines as the day (Psalms 139:12)."*

10. Nor does the descent of level after level prevent His blessed speech from remaining in a state of absolute unity with Him, but it is metaphorically like the snail whose garment is part of him.[23]

11. The error that secular philosophers make which leads them to believe that God created the

---

[23] Genesis Rabba 21

world and then abandoned it to its own devices is that they assume that the creative process of God is the same as that of man. In truth, it is vastly different, as it is written, *"For My thoughts are not like your thoughts,"* and, *"Thus My ways are higher than your ways (Isaiah 55:8-9)."* Man is merely capable of creating something from something. The human craftsman takes an ingot of silver and fashions a vessel from it. When the craftsman removes his hand from his creation, the vessel remains. This is because the craftsman merely changes the form of a created substance. However, when God created the heavens and the earth, He made them from absolute nothingness, and were He to remove His creative force, they would be as they were before He brought them forth into the state of revealed creation, that is, they would be non-existent.[24]

12. From the foregoing words of truth, it should be apparent how the entirety of creation is, in truth,

---

[24] Tanya, Gate of Unity and Faith, chap. 2, pp. 72a-72b

considered null and void with respect to God's activating force and the breath of His mouth. This does not mean that the creation is an illusion. What it means is that God's Divine Force is its true existence and that the creation has no independent existence of its own. However, it must be realized that the example of God's removing His original Ten Saying was hypothetical. God has no such intention. The universe is real. It is, however, nullified to its Creator. How do we know the universe is real? Inasmuch as our limited senses and intellect are part of the created universe, any proof they might offer is inconclusive, for we are part of the very thing that may not exist! There is but one proof that the universe really exists. It says so in the Torah, as it is written *"In the beginning, God created the heavens and the earth (Genesis 1:1)."*

13. The reason that every created being and thing appears to possess an independent self-existence is that we do not grasp or see with our physical eyes the power of God and the breath of His mouth

that is within creation. If permission were granted the eye to see the life force and the spirituality that flow from God to every created thing, then we would no longer see the physicality of material existence. For, since the physical world is truly nullified to its Source, if we could see the Divine source, how could we see the physical world?[25]

14. By analogy, a ray of sunlight may be seen from the earth, but from the perspective of the sun which is the source of the ray, all that is seen is the light that fills the sky. From the sun's perspective, the ray has no existence whatsoever.[26]

15. However, the analogy of the ray of sunlight is incomplete, because its source, the sun, exists only in one place in the heavens. The sun does not exist both in the heavens and on earth where its light appears to have a separate existence. This is

---

[25] Ibid., chap. 3, p.78b
[26] Ibid.

in contrast to created beings, which are always within their Source, although the Source is not revealed to their eyes.[27]

16. It is not sufficient to say that God created the world during the six days of creation, for His creative activity is continuous, an infinite flow of life force. This is why it is written in the present tense, *"He creates darkness and forms light,"*[28] rather than in the past tense – He created darkness and formed light. And this applies to man as well. The man who feels his own self-importance and does not recognize that the Creator is bringing him forth from absolute nothingness into existence is called one whom God created in the past tense. This is in contrast to a person who acknowledges the truth of his existence, realizing that it constantly comes from God alone. This person is called one whom God creates. One who contemplates these

---

[27] Ibid.

[28] Siddur (Hebrew Prayer Book), morning prayer service

teachings will surely come to realize that God is truly our Father and our King Who brings us into being and desires our existence.

Chapter Three

Returning to God

INTRODUCTION

If any single concept exemplifies the knowledge of God, it is Judaism's belief that man can achieve *complete* repentance. Judaism does not even find the word "repentance" sufficient, for repentance presupposes a natural state of sinfulness from which, in reality, there is no complete return. The Jewish concept is called *tshuvah,* return.

Christianity, for example, views man as being a hopeless victim of original sin. In that light, complete repentance is impossible. How can one return to one's pure nature if the pure nature itself is blemished?

In truth, repentance is withheld from the sinner only by his own evil mind and deceitful heart. If he sincerely wishes to draw near to God, the gates of repentance are open to him and no hindrance exists which can prevent him from attaining his goal. On the contrary, God opens the gate of righteousness for all and, in His lovingkindness and goodness, instructs man in the good way, as it is written, *"Good and upright is the Lord; therefore, He will teach sinners the way (Psalms 25:8)."* And it is also written, *"The Lord is close to all who call upon Him in truth" (Psalms 145:18)."*

How can the Christian idea of original sin be acceptable when nine souls have ascended to their eternal reward without experiencing death?[1]

The most notable of these, of course, is the Prophet Elijah who in his body ascended to

---

[1] *Yalkut Shimoni, Ezekiel, chapter 367, section 28.* The nine who entered the Garden of Eden without tasting death are Enoch, Elijah, Messiah, Eliezer the servant of Abraham, Oved the King of Cush, Hiram the King of Tzor, Yaabetz the grandson of Rebbe Judah the Prince, Serah the daughter of Asher, and Batya the daughter of Pharaoh, who adopted Moses. There is an opinion that Rabbi Yehoshua ben Levi is one of the nine instead of Hiram the King of Tzor.

heaven in a flaming chariot (2 Kings 2:11). Another was Serah, the daughter of Asher, who informed her grandfather Jacob that his son Joseph was alive and well in Egypt.[2]

Hasidim teach that the Baal Shem Tov was offered the opportunity to be the tenth to leave this earth without dying, but he chose to experience death.[3] He saw everything as emanating solely from God, therefore ultimately good and worth experiencing, as it says, *"The feet of the Shechina[4] descend even unto death (Prov. 5:5, 7:27)."*

Judaism rejects the notion of being trapped by original sin.[5] We learn that Abraham

---

[2] *Yalkut Me'am Loez,* Genesis, vol. *2,* p. *779*

[3] *Sefer HaArchin Chabad,* vol. 1, pp. *83, 84*

[4] The Divine Revelation of God.

[5] The Oral Tradition teaches that, at Mount Sinai, the Children of Israel attained perfection, rising above death, only to fall again with the sin of the golden calf. It is possible to say, therefore, that Israelites and the Noahides (the rest of mankind) have different sins to overcome to return to the pristine state. Israel must reject idolatry whereas the Noahide is to observe general obedience to God's word to rectify Adam's sin in the Garden of Eden.

and Sara fulfilled what Adam and Eve failed to fulfill.[6] And Jacob, through his exalted service of God, achieved a true rectification of the sin of the Tree of Knowledge of Good and Evil.[7]

This means that man can return to God, no matter how far he has fallen. The method of man's return to his true and sinless state of being is systematically delineated in Judaism and workable by anyone, whether Israelite or Noahide.

Why should man strive to return to God? The simple reason is, of course, to avoid punishment. But there is a nobler reason. Suppose a person had in his possession a great painting by Rembrandt, for example. Not knowing it was a treasured object, he had stored it away in the attic gathering dust and mold. Once he learns that the painting is real and that he has a masterpiece in his possession, the person will

---

[6] *Babylonian Talmud, Baba Batra,* chapter 5

[7] Duties of the Heart, Gate of Repentance, chap. 10

certainly go up to the attic, retrieve the painting, clean it off and restore it to its original state. Is a person's own soul not worthy of a similar honor? For it is said that of all the treasures entrusted to you by your Creator, the one most worthy of honor is your own soul.[8]

PART TWO – *God's kindness to man.*

1. A person must realize that God, Blessed Be He, is more merciful to man than anyone or anything else can be. The Creator, Blessed Be He, does not conceal anything from a person which might improve his personal welfare. Man is God's creation, and no one can better understand how to care for a creation than its original maker. If this principle applies to a human craftsman, who does not create any new form but merely changes the form of an already existing creation, then certainly it is true of God, Who brought man into

---

[8] Ibid., Gate of Trust in God, chap. 3

being from nothingness and sustains him at every instance and every second. God is all-knowing in the ways of what is best for man, what can damage him and what will work to his advantage.[9]

2. One should contemplate and know that God lavishes great and abundant kindness on man. From the beginning of human existence, God has bestowed these kindnesses even without man's being worthy of them or aware of them. And it is not because God has a need for man, but only because of God's great goodness and generosity.[10]

3. One should also realize clearly that God observes him at all times and that there is nothing hidden from Him. All stand revealed before Him. God knows whether or not a person has complete trust in Him. Therefore, it is fitting for a person to trust God and turn to Him, abandoning ways contrary to Him. By observing the Seven Noahide

---

[9] Ibid.

[10] Ibid.

Commandments with care and deliberation, one demonstrates that he has put his complete trust in God. God will then reciprocate with trust in man, leading him to success and happiness in all matters.

4. There is no miracle in the creation as great as returning to God through repentance. Repentance is greater than wisdom. By means of wisdom, man can discriminate between good and evil, choosing the good and rejecting the evil. Nevertheless, the evil remains evil. But through repentance, man has the miraculous power to convert evil into good, for the sins and the remorse of having committed them are the very things that draw a person to God with impassioned longing and great love. Therefore, through repentance, the sins themselves become transformed from evil to good.[11]

---

[11] Shaarei Tshuvah, Rebbe Dov Ber of Lubavitch, chap. 1

5. A Chasidic Rebbe once happened upon a person who was a notorious sinner. The Rebbe walked up to the man and confessed that he was envious of him.

"But Rebbe," the man said, amazed, "you are a saint and I am a sinner. Why should you be envious of me?"

"Because," the Rebbe answered, "you can bring a much greater light into the world than I can. I can only bring goodness to the world by resisting sin and doing what I am supposed to do. You can transform thousands, maybe millions, of evil deeds into wondrous merits by repenting and returning to God."[12]

PART THREE – *Advantages of repentance and how to achieve complete repentance.*

---

[12] Tales of the Chassidim, Zevin, Stories of the Jewish Holidays, p.45

1. If a person has transgressed one or all of the Seven Noahide Commandments, either willfully or unintentionally, when he repents, he is obligated to confess verbally, specifying his sins before the God of kindness, blessed be He. How should he confess? He should speak words to this effect: "I implore You, God, I have sinned unintentionally, willfully, spitefully. I have done thus and so (specify the transgression). I regret my actions and am ashamed of them and will not do thus and so again." This is the essence of confession. Anyone who increases the content of his confession and elaborates upon it is praiseworthy.[13]

2. The punishment imposed on a person by a Noahide court of law serves as an atonement for the transgression if the person confesses his sins to God in the above manner.

---

[13] Mishneh Torah, Laws of Repentance, 1:1

If one injures a friend or causes him monetary loss, even if he has paid back what he owes, he has not atoned for his transgression until he confesses to God and resolves never to repeat such a deed again.

3. Repentance atones for all sins. Even if one is evil all the days of his life and returns to God on the last day, none of his wickedness is mentioned to him in the Divine Judgment.[14]

4. What is complete repentance? If, after having confessed, it occurs to the person to repeat the transgression done in the past. And if the opportunity to repeat the transgression presents itself, but he resists and refrains from doing it solely because of repentance and not because of his fear of anyone (for example, the police), and not because he is too weak physically and can no longer do it, then he has achieved complete repentance.

---

[14] Ibid., 1:3

For example, if a man has had a forbidden relationship with a woman and he has repented and confessed, and after a time it happens that he finds himself alone with her again,[15] and now he resists and does not transgress, this person has accomplished complete repentance.[16]

5. If a person returns to God, repenting of his transgressions only in his old age, at a time of life when he is no longer able to repeat the transgressions of the past, although this is not the highest form of repentance, he is still considered a true penitent who has returned to God.

6. Even if one transgresses all his life and repents the day of his death and dies a penitent, all his sins are forgiven. Thus, if one remembers his Creator and returns to Him before he dies, he is forgiven.

---

[15] Or in a similar circumstance with a different woman.
[16] Ibid., 2:1

7. And what is repentance? It is the sinner's abandonment of his sin, removing it from his thoughts, resolving not to do it again. Consequently, he regrets what has happened in the past and accepts God, the Knower of secrets, as his Witness that he will never return to such a sin again. And he must confess verbally the resolutions that he made in his heart.[17]

8. One who confesses with words and does not resolve in his heart to leave his sin is like one who immerses in a *mikvah* (ritual purification pool) while holding a dead rat in his hand. The immersion in the pool brings no purification until he discards the unclean object.[18]

9. On the path of repentance, the penitent should cry to God with tears and supplications and give charity according to his capability, at least ten percent of his income and preferably twenty

---

[17] Ibid., 2:2
[18] Ibid., 2:3

percent.[19] He should also distance himself from the thing in which he sinned or the person with whom he sinned, or even the place wherein he committed the sin. He should change all his deeds and tread a straight path, and he should exile himself from his present residence since exile is atonement because it brings a person to humility, and the essence of repentance comes through a broken heart and a humble spirit.[20]

10. It is praiseworthy for the penitent to confess publicly, even to the extent of informing others of his transgressions, saying to his peers, "I sinned against so-and-so and I have done such-and-such. But I have changed my ways and deeply regret my past."[21]

---

[19] A person will spend all his money to save his life medically, how much more so to safeguard his eternal soul.

[20] Ibid., 2:4

[21] Ibid., 2:5

11. One who is haughty and will not inform others of his transgressions, choosing to conceal them, does not attain complete repentance.

12. Public declaration refers to the sins between oneself and his fellow man. The sins that are between oneself and his Creator need not be broadcast, and, in fact, it is considered the ultimate of brazenness to reveal them, as it shows that the person is not embarrassed about them. Let him simply return to God, blessed be He, specifying his sins before Him. Any public confession should be in a general way without specifying actions, and he should consider it a blessing that his iniquity has not become revealed.

13. The above mentioned formula of repentance helps only with sins that one commits between himself and God. For sins that are between

oneself and his fellow man, he has to pacify his fellow and ask forgiveness from him.[22]

14. If a person receives an apology, he should never refuse to be pacified, but should forgive easily and be slow to feel anger toward another. At the time someone asks forgiveness of him, he should grant favor with a full heart and a sincere spirit.

15. Every person should consider himself perfectly balanced between reward and punishment. Similarly, he should see the entire world as balanced with respect to his deeds. If he commits one sin, he tilts the scales of judgment for himself and for the entire world toward guilt and condemnation, and consequently he can be the cause of the whole world's destruction. But if he does one good deed, he tilts the scales of judgment

---

[22] Ibid.

toward merit and can bring salvation and deliverance for himself and the whole world.[23]

PART FOUR – *The concept of free will.*

1. The power of self-determination is given to every person. If one wants to direct himself toward goodness and righteousness, the power is in his hand; if he wants to direct himself to the way of evil, the power is similarly his.[24]

2. Man is unique in this world, and there is no other creation that can compare to him in this regard. Man is intellectually aware of good and evil. He does what he wishes to do, and no one can prevent him from choosing to do good or evil.

3. One should banish the idea that fools speak about, that God has decreed man's destiny from birth whether he will be righteous or wicked.

---

[23] Ibid., 3:4
[24] Ibid., 5:2

There is no such thing. Every person has the ability to become righteous or wicked, compassionate or cruel, generous or selfish. And so it is with all other character traits and abilities to live within the normative conduct set for man by the commandments of God.[25]

It is true, however, that the individual may be born with tendencies toward specific problematic behavior, but at all times it is within his power to overcome these natural tendencies. No one is born a thief or a sexual deviant.[26]

4. If God had predetermined the individual's destiny, whether for good or for evil, on what basis could the righteous be rewarded and the wicked be punished? Just as the Creator desired that fire and wind should naturally rise upward, and water and earth should naturally descend, and that a planet should move in a circular motion, and all other creatures of the world should act in accord

---

[25] *Sicha of* the Lubavitcher Rebbe, Purim *5746 (1986)*

[26] *Mishneh Torah,* Laws of Repentance, chapter *5,* law *4*

with the nature that God chose for them, thus did God desire that man should have the free will to determine his actions.[27]

5. Therefore, man is judged according to his deeds. If he does good, he is repaid with good. If he does evil, he earns a payment of evil. And at a future time, he must surrender himself to judgment for his thoughts, speech, and actions. The person who fulfills the Seven Noahide Commandments, and thereby does good in this world, is repaid with boundless good from God.

6. The reward for doing good is hundreds of times greater than the punishment for doing evil, for it is written, *"I, the Lord your God, am a jealous God, visiting the iniquity of the fathers upon the children unto the third and fourth generation of them that hate Me; and showing mercy for two thousand generations of them that love Me and keep My commandments (Exodus 20:5-6)."*

---

[27] Ibid., 6:1

PART FIVE – *Divine Providence and the individual, his fortunes being dependent on his deeds; the methods of achieving repentance.*

1. Whenever a person commits a transgression with his own knowledge and will, it is proper that he be punished for it so that he is repaid for his deeds. God knows exactly how he should be paid. The judgment may be that the sinner should be punished in this world with afflictions of the body through illness or physical damage. The punishment might take the form of loss of property and wealth, or the sinner's children might be afflicted because of his wrongdoings.

Also, there are sins that are judged to be repaid in the World to Come rather than harm befalling the transgressor in this world. And there are sins that must be paid for both in this world and in the World to Come.[28]

---

[28] Ibid., 6:2

2. One should consider it a great kindness to be punished in this world, for the World to Come is eternal and all aspects of it are eternal. This reveals a glimmer of understanding of why the righteous appear to suffer and the wicked prosper. It is as if God says of the wicked, "The little good he did in this world I will repay him in this world so that there remains no reward for him in the Eternal World, but the payment for his sins awaits him in full measure." And of the righteous, it is as if God says, "For his few sins I will punish him in this world, where afflictions are transitory, and for his great number of merits I will withhold reward in this world so that I can bestow upon him the greatest possible measure of eternal good in the World to Come."

3. When we speak of a man paying for his wicked deeds, this presumes that he does not repent and abandon them. But if he repents, it is considered a shield between him and the punishment. And just as a man sins with his own understanding

and free will, he can also repent through his own understanding and free will.[29]

4. There is a circumstance in which God does not offer a person the opportunity to repent. When a person commits an extremely grave sin or an overwhelming number of sins with his own understanding and free will,[30] the opportunity to abandon his evil is not granted to him in order that he should be lost in the sins that he committed.

However, this merely means that repentance is made difficult for the person. Nevertheless, it is written that nothing can stand between a man and repentance, and a person can always overcome the obstacles and through strength of will return to God in full repentance.[31]

---

[29] Ibid., 6:3

[30] Such as causing others to sin by leading them to idolatry or by murdered large numbers of people through acts of terror.

[31] Ibid., 7:2

5. A person should constantly regard himself as being close to death, and finding himself standing in sin, he should immediately repent from all his sins. He should not say, "When I grow older, I will repent." Perhaps he will die before he reaches old age.[32]

6. One should not say that repentance applies only to sins involving actual deeds, such as forbidden sexual relations and theft. For just as a man must repent of those, he must become introspective concerning his undesirable character traits and repent of them, from his anger and his hatred and from jealousy and folly and from pursuit of wealth and honor and excessive gluttony and other base attributes. He must withdraw from all of them and return to God. One who is accustomed to destructive pursuits and evil traits finds it more difficult to abandon severe sins involving actual evil deeds.[33]

---

[32] Ibid., 7:3

[33] Ibid., 7:4

7. A true penitent should not worry that as a result of his sins he is a long way from the exalted status of righteousness. The truth is that he is loved and treasured by the Creator as if he had never committed a sin. Moreover, when he repents, his reward is enormous: he has tasted sin and departed from it, and has conquered his evil inclination. This makes him far greater than one who has never tasted sin, for the penitent has achieved a greater spiritual conquest.[34]

8. The ways of the penitent should be humble and modest. If fools and boors taunt him about his previous deeds and say to him, "Yesterday you were doing such-and-such, and now look at you trying to be so high and mighty," he should pay no attention to them, but listen silently and rejoice and know that their insults are bringing him even greater merit. When a penitent is embarrassed about his past deeds and is humiliated because of

---

[34] Ibid., 7:8

them, his merits are increased and his spiritual level is exalted all the more.[35]

9. It is a grave sin to say to a penitent, "Remember your previous deeds," or to mention anything of his past ways in order to embarrass him, or to mention ideas or incidents that will remind him of what he has done.

10. Great is repentance, for it draws a person close to God, and the further one's distance, the closer and more beloved one can become through repentance. "Yesterday he was despicable in front of God, disgusting, alienated, an abomination. And today, he is precious, close, and beloved."[36]

PART SIX – *Payment in the World to Come.*

1. The treasure reserved for the righteous is eternal life in the World to Come. This is a life

---

[35] Ibid., 7:6
[36] Ibid., 8:1

that does not incorporate death. It is goodness that does not co-exist with evil. The punishment for the wicked is that they do not merit this life, but will be cut off and perish completely. All who do not merit this eternal life are considered truly dead. The wicked are expunged in their wickedness and perish like animals. This means that the wicked person whose soul is cut off from the body by spiritual extinction does not merit the eternal life of the World to Come.[37]

2. Loss of the life of the World to Come is the most dreadful retribution, for it is total loss and a complete destruction. It is a loss than can never be regained because repentance and return to God can be achieved only while the soul is in the body in this material world. Once the soul has departed from the body, the time for good deeds or wicked deeds or repentance has passed. It is then the time for reward or punishment.[38]

---

[37] Ibid., 8:5

[38] Ibid., 8:6

3. There are certain misguided people who imagine that the reward for obeying God's commandments and for following the way of truth is to inherit a paradise where they are able to eat and drink sumptuous foods and beverages, to enjoy relationships with "beautiful forms," to wear linen and brocaded garments, to dwell in ivory palaces and use vessels of gold and silver, and other similar fantasies. The intelligent among mankind will easily see that these images are foolish and vain, and that there is neither inner purpose nor spiritual meaning to them. These ideas betray a lack of understanding and a compulsion for physicality, for it is merely because we have physical bodies that these things have any meaning.

All of these dreams of sensory delights are attractive only to the body; the soul has no desire for them. The soul desires to fulfill bodily needs only so as to establish and maintain health, and takes no pleasure in physical delights at all.[39]

4. In the time of the eternal life where there is no body or any physical existence at all, these material things will be entirely nullified. There, in the World to Come, the great goodness is for the soul alone. And there is no way in this world to attain any comprehension of this pleasure whatsoever, for the delights of the World to Come are glorious beyond human concept, and there is nothing of this world to compare to their supernal goodness.

5. The sages of Israel call it the World to Come not because it will exist in a future time and cannot be found here and now, but because it is the life that comes to man after the physical life of this world where the soul is encased in a physical body.

---

[39] Ibid., 8:8

The World to Come exists now and can be found now. It is found as it has been found from the very beginning.[40]

6. We are commanded to walk the middle path for it is the good and proper way, as it says, *"You should walk in His ways" (Deuteronomy 30:16)."* Just as God is called gracious, man must be gracious. Just as God is called merciful, man must be merciful. Man is obligated to follow the ways of God to the fullest extent of his ability.[41]

7. A person can accustom himself to this manner of conduct by performing deeds that reflect moderation, repeating them constantly until they become ingrained and established traits. And because these traits are called names such as gracious, merciful, kind, righteous, which the Creator is called, this way of the middle path is

---

[40] Ibid.

[41] Ibid., The Book of Knowledge 1:6

called the way of God. Whoever walks this path brings goodness and blessing upon him or her.[42]

8. This middle path is a striving for moderation in all things, in physical pleasures, emotional expression, even in intellectual and spiritual pursuits. The parable is given of a religious man who discovers that by withdrawing from a certain physical pleasure, he automatically feels closer to God. So what does he do? He acts in the extreme, becoming a hermit, denying himself everything of this world, denying himself anything of human existence. It does not take long before he degenerates to a level of inhumanity like a wild animal, further from God than when he began his spiritual journey. We can understand the cause of his failure by considering two men, one with a gold coin and the other with a million gold coins. Obviously, the man with a million gold coins has

---

[42] The Ramban's Letter to his son. Ramban is an acronym for Rabbi Moses ben Nachman (1194-1270), a great halachic authority and kabbalist, and author of one of the primary commentaries to the Five Books of Moses.

999,999 more than the man with one. Now consider the case of three men, one with one gold coin, a second with a million gold coins, and a third with infinite gold coins. Who is closer to the one with infinite gold coins, the man with one or the man with a million? They are both exactly the same distance away since there is no relationship whatsoever between the finite of any number and the infinite. So it is with all fields of human endeavor. Man is a finite being with limited intellect, limited emotions, limited physical strength. God is infinite. There is no way that man, by using his own reason and power, can approach the Creator. This is why the hermit's conclusion, logical as it may have seemed, failed him. Man can approach the Infinite only by following the method prescribed for him by the Infinite, and the method prescribed is the way of moderation, the middle path.

9. There are exceptions. When it comes to anger or false pride, one should strive to avoid these destructive traits to the ultimate. Anger is

controlled and ultimately eliminated by speaking gently to all people at all times and in all situations.[43] And pride is circumvented by realizing that one is nothing and achieves nothing except for what God bestows as a gift. Another exception to clinging to the middle path is what is called *shtiyot d'kedusha,* the folly of holiness. This means that man, finding himself in the situation of being sunk in the pursuit of physical pleasures, even permissible physical pleasures, should temporarily act in the opposite extreme to counter the situation and eventually achieve moderation.[44]

10. In order to assure success in one's strivings, it is important to select a respected friend as both a consultant and a confidant. When matters of doubt or concern arise pertaining to performance

---

[43] The Ramban's Letter to his Son. Ramban is an acronym for Rabbi Moses ben Nachman (1194-1270), a great halachic authority and kabbalist, and author of one of the primary commentaries to the Five Books of Moses.

[44] Mishneh Torah, the Book of Knowledge 2:3; Bati L'Gani maamar, p. 4

of the Seven Laws of Noah, another person's assessment of the situation can provide objectivity in determining the appropriate course of action. This is called, *aseh lecha rav* – find a teacher for yourself.[45]

This spiritual "buddy system" will expand one's perspective and clarity, objectives that can be met even if the advisor is less than a towering genius or spiritual giant. What is desired here is the ability to open up in a sincere dialogue.

11. Every person on the earth whose spirit is humble and who differentiates between good and evil in order to be able to stand before God, to serve Him and know Him and walk upright in His path, removing the yoke of the scheming and calculating with which most people conduct their lives, sanctifies the Holy of Holies. God will be this person's portion and inheritance in this world and the World to Come forever and ever. And he will

---

[45] Chapters of the Fathers, 1:6

merit success in all his material efforts in this world. As it is written, *"Seek the Lord while He may be found; call upon Him while He is near"* *(Isaiah 55:6)."*[46]

---

[46] Mishneh Torah, Laws of Sabbatical and Jubilee Years, 13:13

Chapter Four

The Seven Laws of Noah

1. With respect to God's commandments, all of humanity is divided into two general classifications: the Children of Israel and the Children of Noah.

2. The Children of Israel are the Jewish people, the descendants of the Patriarch Jacob. They are commanded to fulfill the 613 Commandments of the Torah.

3. The Children of Noah comprise the seventy original nations of the world and their branches. They are commanded concerning the Seven Universal Commandments which are known as the Seven Laws of Noah.[1] These seven universal laws are the elementary and basic principles of civilized humanity. The seven laws pertain to idolatry, blasphemy, murder, theft, forbidden sexual relations, eating the limb of a living animal, and establishing courts of law.

---

[1] Babylonian Talmud, Sanhedrin 56a

4. All Seven Universal Laws are prohibitions.[2] Do not wonder at this. Negative commandments are of a higher order than positive commandments, and their fulfillment, which takes more effort than positive commandments, earns a greater reward.

5. Men and women are equal in their responsibility to observe these seven commandments.[3]

6. It is a matter of dispute as to when a person becomes responsible for his or her actions under these laws. One opinion holds that it depends on the intellectual development of the individual.[4] According to this opinion, as soon as a child has attained the maturity to understand the meaning and significance of the Seven Universal Laws,[5] he is obligated to the fullest extent of the law.

---

[2] The Ramban lists establishing Courts of Law as a positive command.

[3] *Encyclopedia Talmudica,* The Children of Noah, volume 3, page 348

[4] Rabbeinu Asher (the Rosh), responsa number 16

[5] This is known as a *"bar daat,"* a child of knowledge, i.e., one whose intellectual development is sufficient for him or her to make reasonable choices.

The other opinion is that a boy reaches the age of legal responsibility at his thirteenth birthday and a girl at her twelfth birthday.[6]

7. The Children of Noah are permanently warned concerning the Seven Universal Laws. This means that ignorance of the law is not a valid defense. One cannot claim, for example, that he did not know that idolatry was one of the seven commandments. Nor can he claim that he did not know that bowing down to an idol constitutes idolatry.[7] Therefore, one is duty bound to study the Seven Universal Laws to the best of one's ability and to teach the knowledge of them to one's children.

8. When one of the Children of Noah resolves to fulfill the Seven Universal Laws, his or her soul is elevated. This person becomes one of the *Chasidei Umot ha-Olam,* the Pious Ones of the Nations, and receives a share of the Eternal World.[8] The Talmud call one who accepts the

---

[6] *Babylonian Talmud, Nazir* 29b, commentary of Rashi: "And Rabbi Yose…"; *Likutei Sichot,* volume 5, page 421

[7] However, he can claim that he did not realize that a certain idol was an idol, for that is not ignorance of the law.

[8] Mishneh Torah, Laws of Kings, 8:11; Talmud Bavli, Avodah Zara 64b

yoke of fulfilling the Seven Universal Laws a *ger toshav,* a foreign resident. This person is permitted to live in the Land of Israel and to enter the Holy Temple in Jerusalem and to offer sacrifices to the God of Israel.[9]

9. Although the Children of Noah are commanded only concerning the Seven Universal Laws, they are permitted to observe any of the 613 Commandments of the Torah for the sake of receiving divine reward.[10] According to some opinions the exceptions to this are:

> A. Observing the Sabbath in the manner of the Jews. This means that the Children of Noah may not completely rest from the 39 creative work activities that were needed for the building of the Tabernacle during the Exodus from Egypt. This is a complicated subject whose details and implications are outside the scope of this book, but will be addressed at greater length in a later work.

---

[9] Ibid., Laws of Forbidden Relationships, 14:7

[10] Ibid., 64b; Mishneh Torah, Laws of Kings, 10:9.

B. Observing the Jewish holy days in the manner of the Jews. This also means resting from the creative work activities in a similar manner to the Sabbath.[11]

C. Studying those parts of the Torah that do not apply to the Noahides' service of God. This prohibition, like the others, may apply to some Children of Noah and not others.[12]

D. Writing a Torah scroll comprised of the Five Books of Moses.

E. Receiving an *aliyah* to the Torah.[13]

Note: A prime purpose of the Seven Universal Laws is to teach the Children of Noah about the Oneness of God. Therefore, it is permissible and even

---

[11] There are several fundamental differences between resting on the Sabbath and resting on a Jewish holiday. A full discussion of these details and implications will similarly be included in a later work.

[12] The Rambam in the Mishneh Torah forbids these categories to the "acum," a term for an idol worshipper, literally meaning one who worships stars and constellations. This would indicate that a Noahide who has elevated his soul by accepting the Seven Laws may well be permitted to engage in Torah study, Shabbat observances, etc.

[13] Being called up to a communal reading of selected portions of the Torah.

imperative that he acquire this knowledge from Torah study. This includes the entire twenty-four books of the Hebrew Scriptures. Also, the study of any part of the Torah that brings one to greater knowledge concerning the performance of the Seven Noahide Commandments is permissible.

Talmudic or Halakhic study of subjects that pertain exclusively to the Jew's service of God is expressly forbidden to an *acum*,[14] i.e., a Noahide who worships idols and is, therefore, not one of the *Chasidei Umot Haolam (Pious Gentile)*. The *acum* damages his soul if he studies portions of the Torah that do not pertain to him.[15]

10. A Noahide who, though forbidden, engages in learning Torah or observes the Sabbath in the manner of Jews, or reveals novel meanings to verses in the Torah, may be physically restrained and informed that he is liable

---

[14] A full discussion of Scriptural and Talmudic terminology will be included in a later work.

[15] Sicha of the Lubavitcher Rebbe, 19th Kislev 5745 (1984)

for capital punishment by divine decree, but he is not put to death by a court of law.

Note: The action taken against this person is only meant to dissuade him from doing forbidden acts.

11. The responsibility of The Seven Noahide Laws is a yoke of faith in God. This means that the laws must be observed solely because God commanded them. If the Children of Noah observe these Seven Universal Laws for any reason or intention other than to fulfill God's will, no divine reward for the performance is received. This means that if one of the Children of Noah says, "These laws seem sensible and beneficial, therefore I will observe them," his actions accomplish nothing spiritually. He is not a *Ger Toshav* (Resident Foreigner) nor is he considered one of the *Chasidei Umot HaOlam*.[16]

12. A Noahide who studies Torah is comparable to the High Priest of the Jews, for both are rewarded with a share of the World to Come.[17]

---

[16] Mishneh Torah, Laws of Kings, 8:11

[17] Babylonian Talmud, Baba Kamma, 38a

13. If one of the Children of Noah wishes to accept the full responsibility of the 613 Commandments of the Torah, he or she can convert and become a Jew in every respect. One who elects to do this is called a *Ger Tzedek,* a righteous proselyte.[18]

It is a principle of Judaism, however, not to seek converts, and one who requests conversion is generally discouraged. Should the person persist in the desire to convert, counsel should be taken only with an Orthodox rabbi or scholar, for conversion not in accord with *Halakha,* Jewish Law, is no conversion at all, and conversion supervised and granted by rabbis who themselves do not follow the laws of the Torah are null and void, neither recognized in heaven nor by any God-fearing Jew.

14. It is incorrect to think that since the Children of Israel have 613 Commandments and the Children of Noah have seven commandments, the ratio of spiritual worth is proportionally 613 to 7. The truth is that the Seven Universal Laws are general commandments, each

---

[18] *Shulchan Arukh, Yoreh Deah,* Laws of Conversion, chapter 268, law 2

containing many parts and details, whereas the 613 Commandments of the Torah are specific, each relating to one basic detail of the Divine Law. Therefore, the numerical disparity in no way reflects the relative spiritual worth of the two systems of commandments.[19]

The prime difference in the service of the Israelite and that of the Noahide is that the Noahide sees the existence of existence, that is, he refines the world, whereas the Israelite sees the non-existence of existence, that is, he reveals divinity in the world. Of course, refining the world reveals its inherent divinity and revealing divinity inevitably refines the world.

15. The statutory penalty for intentionally transgressing any one of the Seven Laws of Noah is capital punishment.[20]

A Noahide who inadvertently violates one of his commandments is exempt from punishment. The sole exception is a person who murders unwittingly but

---

[19] *The Seven Laws of Noah,* Lichtenstein, chapter 9, page 89

[20] Mishneh Torah, Laws of Kings, 9:14. This is the opinion of the Rambam. The subject will be discussed more fully in Chapter 11, Courts of Law

negligently. Although the courts will not punish the killer for manslaughter, he may be killed by a blood redeemer. The blood redeemer is someone close to the slain party who seeks retribution. The blood redeemer in turn will not be killed for his actions.[21] According to others, in the case of murder, a transgressor of the Noahide Law who is ignorant of the law, but acted negligently, receives the death penalty in a court of law.

16. If the courts cannot punish an individual for lack of witnesses or any other reason, the transgressor will be punished from heaven by divine decree.[22]

17. Besides the Seven Universal Commandments, the Children of Noah have traditionally taken it upon themselves to fulfill the commandment of honoring father and mother.[23]

18. Some authorities are of the opinion that the Children of Noah are obligated to fulfill the commandment of

---

[21] Ibid., 10:1

[22] Commentary of Rashi on Exodus 23:7 and 21:13; *Babylonian Talmud, Sanhedrin* 37b

[23] *Nahal Eshkol,* Laws of Circumcision, chapter 39, number 6

giving charity.[24] Others state that it is proper and meritorious for the Children of Noah to give charity but that it is not actually commanded of them.[25]

19. If a Noahide who follows the Seven Universal Laws gives charity, the Israelites accept it from him and give it to the poor of Israel. Through the merit of giving charity to the Jewish poor, one is given life by God and saved from death. But if a Noahide does not accept the yoke of the Seven Noahide Laws, but remains an *acum* and gives charity, it may not be given it to the needy of Israel. His charity is given to poor Noahides only.[26]

20. If one of the Children of Noah arises and performs a miracle and says that God sent him, then instructs others to add to or subtract from any of the Seven Universal Laws or explains them in a way not heard at Mount Sinai, or claims that the 613 Commandments given to the Jews are not eternal, but limited to a fixed period of time, this

---

[24] *Babylonian Talmud, Sanhedrin* 56b, commentary of Rabbeinu Nissim, "And He commanded him - these are the judges"

[25] Mishneh Torah, Laws of Kings, 10:10

[26] Ibid.

person is deemed a false prophet and incurs the death penalty.[27]

21. There is an oral tradition that the Children of Noah are forbidden to interbreed animals of different species or to graft trees of different kinds,[28] although some authorities hold that they are permitted to do either.[29] However, they may wear *shaatnez*[30] and they may plant different seeds such as grape and wheat in the same field, which are acts forbidden to Jews.[31] Forbidden interbreeding and grafting are not punishable in courts of law.

22. The Sages of Israel state that descendants of the children of Ketura, the sons of Abraham's concubine, Hagar, who were born after Ishmael and Isaac, must by law be circumcised. Since today the descendants of Ishmael are intermixed with the descendants of the other sons of Hagar, all are obligated to be circumcised on the

---

[27] Ibid., Foundations of Torah, 9:1

[28] Ibid., 10:6

[29] *Shulchan Arukh, Yoreh Deah,* chapter 297, note 3, commentary of the *Shach*

[30] Clothing containing both wool and linen.

[31] Babylonian Talmud, Sanhedrin 56b

eighth day after they are born. Those transgressing this are not liable for the death penalty.[32] This law applies to Semitic peoples, although all other nations are allowed to circumcise if they desire.

23. One opinion maintains that only the six sons of Hagar and not their descendants were obligated to be circumcised.[33]

24. In accord with the Seven Universal Laws, mankind is enjoined against creating any religion based on his own concept. He either develops religion based on this Divine Code of Laws or becomes a righteous proselyte, a Jew, and accepts all 613 commandments of the Torah.[34]

Note: Concerning making holidays for themselves, Noahides may participate in the celebration of Jewish holidays, such as Shavuot, celebrating the Giving of the Torah, since the Children of Noah received their commandments at the same time, or Rosh Hashanah, the Jewish New Year and Day of Judgment, since all

---

[32] *Mishneh Torah,* Laws of Kings, chapter 10, law 7, 8

[33] *Babylonion Talmud, Sanhedrin* 59b, commentary of Rashi, "And if you want to say circumcision…"

[34] Babylonian Talmud, Baba Kamma 38a

mankind is judged by God on that day, so it should therefore be important to the Noahide as well as the Israelite. Rosh Hashanah is also the day that Adam, the First Man, was created by God, and all mankind is descended from Adam just as it is from Noah.[35] The Noahide celebrates these holidays in order to bring additional merit and reward to himself.

Moreover, the Noahide is strictly forbidden to create a new holiday that has religious significance and claim that it is part of his religion, even if the religion relates to the Seven Noahide Laws.

For example, it would be forbidden to make a holiday celebrating the subsiding of the waters of the Great Flood or anything similar. All the more so, it is forbidden to institute holidays that ascribe religious significance to events unrelated to the Seven Noahide Laws. Celebrating secular activities and commemorating historical events, even if they involve a festive meal, are permissible.

---

[35] *Me'am Loez*, Genesis, chapter 13, page 194

25. The nations of the world acknowledge the existence of God and essentially do not transgress the will of God. Their failing is an inability to be nullified to God, and they deny His Oneness by thinking that they themselves are separate entities, calling Him the God of gods. Therefore, we find that when they transgress the Seven Noahide Commandments, it is only because a spirit of folly enters them and covers the truth, concealing it from them.[36] But from their essential being, they are not able to transgress the Will of God. Therefore, even Balaam, the wicked prophet who had sexual relations with his donkey, a clear transgression of the Seven Noahide Laws, said, "*I am not able to transgress the word of God (Numbers 22:18)*."

26. The commandment to be fruitful and multiply was given to Noah, but inasmuch as it was not repeated at Mount Sinai, this commandment is not considered part of the Seven Universal Laws.[37]

However, the Children of Noah have the obligation to make the entire earth a dwelling place for

---

[36] *Sefer HaArchin Chabad,* volume 2, The Nations of the World, chapter 1, section *3,* page 269

[37] *Babylonian Talmud, Sanhedrin* 59b

mankind.[38] This is minimally achieved by every couple giving birth to a male and a female child who are in turn capable of reproduction.[39]

A couple that bears more children is credited with bringing more spiritual goodness into the world, assuming that these children are reared in an environment of morality by observing the Seven Universal Laws.

27. A Noahide who strikes an Israelite, causing even a slight wound, though he is theoretically condemned for this, does not receive the death penalty.[40]

28. When a Noahide dies, he is to be buried in the earth, *"for out of it were you taken; for you are dust and unto dust you shall return" (Genesis 3:19)."* This does not mean that a Noahide transgresses one of the Seven Commandments by utilizing another process such as cremation or cryogenic preservation, but he or she will lack the atonement that burial in the earth accomplishes.[41]

---

[38] Sefer HaChinuch, First Commandment

[39] *Shulchan Arukh, Even HaEzer,* chapter 1, law 5

[40] Mishneh Torah, Laws of Kings, 10:6

[41] *Babylonian Talmud, Sanhedrin* 46b

29. By observing the Seven Universal Laws, mankind is given the means by which it can perfect itself. The individual, through these laws and the pathway they open for him, has the power to refine his essential being, reaching higher and higher without limit.

It was taught in the school of Elijah the Prophet, *"I call heaven and earth to bear witness, that any individual, man or woman, Jew or Gentile, freeman or slave, can have the Holy Spirit bestowed upon him. It all depends on his deeds."*[42]

King Solomon, the wisest of men, wrote, *"Ultimately, all is understood: fear God and observe His commandments, for this is the completion of man (Ecclesiastes 12:13)."*

---

[42] Tana D'Bei Eliyahu, beginning of Chapter 9.

Chapter Five

Idolatry

PART ONE: *Definition of idolatry.*

1. The essence of the Seven Laws of Noah is the prohibition against idolatry. One who worships another deity besides the God of Abraham, Creator of heaven and earth, denies the essence of religion and rejects the entirety of the Seven Universal Laws. And one who guards himself against idolatry demonstrates belief in God and affirms the entirety of the Seven Universal Laws.[1]

2. The commandment prohibiting idolatry teaches that one should not serve a created thing – no angel, no plant, no star, nothing of the four fundamentals, earth, water, fire, and air, nor anything that is formulated from them.[2]

---

[1] *Mishneh Torah,* Laws of Idolatry, chapter 2, law 4

[2] Among those things formed of the four fundamental elements is man. The worship of any man, in the flesh, before the flesh, or after the flesh is idol worship.

Even if the worshiper knows that God is the Supreme Being and worships some creation as a way of glorifying God's greatness and His ability to create great beings and things, nevertheless this is idol worship.[3]

3. A person may ponder the heavenly spheres and observe that they do not die like other things and that it is therefore proper to bow down to them and serve them. To do this is to place them between oneself and the Creator. For although God may have assigned these celestial beings certain roles in the conduct of the world, nevertheless, man's responsibilities are to God and not to God's messengers. This, in fact, is how idolatry came to exist in the world.

The generations that lived immediately after Adam recognized that God had created magnificent heavenly beings, the sun to rule by day and the moon to rule by night. And these people began to honor God's exalted messengers.

Soon it was forgotten that these messengers had been appointed by the Creator, and the sun and the moon

---

[3] Ibid., 2:1

began to be honored for their own greatness. This devolved to the worship of these creations as deities themselves without awareness of the God who had created them.[4]

4. Although there are opinions which state that the Children of Noah transgress the prohibition of idolatry from the moment they make an idol, the final law is that the transgression does not come into effect until a Noahide actually worships or serves the idol.[5]

5. According to many authorities, a Noahide is not warned against the concept of "partnership with God."[6]

The concept of partnership is the acknowledgment of the existence of the God of Israel in combination with belief in the possibility and existence of a deity (independent will) other than God. So long as ascribing power to a deity other than the Creator remains conceptual, it is permissible to the Children of Noah

---

[4] Ibid., 1:1

[5] *Babylonian Talmud, Sanhedrin* 56b; *Mishneh Torah,* Laws of Kings, chapter 9, law 2

[6] *Shulchan Arukh, Orach Chaim,* chapter 156, law 1

according to many authorities.[7] But any worship of this independent being is clearly idolatry.

The danger of the concept of partnership is that it frees people to act in accord with non-existent gods and opens a doorway to actual idolatry.

Most recent authorities agree that Noahides are forbidden to believe in a partnership. But even according to this opinion a Noahide is permitted to swear by the name of an idol in combination with God (to swear by the Lord of Hosts and a Hindu deity, for example).

6. The Children of Noah are not commanded to sanctify God's Name by refusing to bow to an idol in the face of a threat to their lives.[8] And there is a dispute whether the Children of Noah are even allowed to choose to lay down their lives in this manner, since they are not commanded to do so.[9] However, since the Children of Noah may perform any of the 613 Commandments of the Torah to receive reward (with the possible exceptions that are

---

[7] *Nodah B'Yehudah,* volume 2, *Yoreh Deah,* number 148

[8] *Mishneh Torah,* Laws of Kings, 10:2

[9] *Babylonian Talmud, Sanhedrin* 74b and 75a; *Tosefos* on 75a

found in the previous chapter), then it would follow that a Noahide may choose to lay down his life for the sanctification of God's Name rather than bow to an idol, even though not commanded to do so.

7. Many books have been written by idol worshipers concerning the nature of their idolatry, the service, procedures, and laws. These teachings may include fascinating philosophy concerning their idolatry. One is advised not to read these books at all, nor should one think about them or speak of them.

Even studying the form of an idolatrous figure or asking how some god is served without having the intention of serving it might cause one to be led to engage in idolatrous practices.[10]

8. Anyone who acknowledges that an idolatrous religion is true, even though he does not serve the idol, insults the mighty and exalted Name of God.[11]

---

[10] *Mishneh Torah,* Laws of Idolatry, 2:2

[11] Ibid., 2:6

PART TWO: *Serving an idol; making an idol.*

1. There are many different types of idolatrous service and the service of one idol is not like the service of another. For example, the ancient idol Peor[12] was served by man's defecating before it.

Note: This bizarre form of worship came about in a degenerative way, similar to the growth of idolatry itself. Originally, worshipers of this idol attained so great a state of ecstasy that they lost control of themselves and defecated. Their children saw the effect and, misunderstanding the cause, concluded that the worship was defecation. The lesson from this remains important today. That a religious rite feels good is no proof of a religion's truth or validity.

2. A person transgresses only when he worships the idol in the normal manner ascribed to each respective idol. Consequently, courts of law have to know the appropriate service for the idol in any case of idolatry.

---

[12] See Deuteronomy 4:3.

3. The preceding law applies to unique forms of worship. If, however, the person bows down or offers sacrifices or incense or a drink offering (the four forms of service of the Holy Temple in Jerusalem) to any one of the idols, he incurs the death penalty even though this may not be the way of that idol's official worship.[13]

4. Food placed upon an altar as an offering to an idol is forbidden to be eaten.[14]

There is a difference of opinion concerning the permissibility of eating food that is unlikely to be offered to an idol, such as a grasshopper or a cockroach.[15]

5. Things such as water and salt, which are not normally in the category of offerings to an idol, are forbidden if they are found directly in front of an idol or within the curtains that surround the idol.

---

[13] Ibid., 3:3

[14] *Chochmat Adam,* Laws of Idolatry, chapter 84, law 6

[15] *Mishneh Torah,* Laws of Idolatry, 3:4

6. It is forbidden to honor an idol even by offering things to it outside the boundaries that surround the idol. This is considered decorating the idol.

Throwing coins at an idol or even into a pool of water next to an idol, such as the statues of oriental gods and demigods commonly seen today, would appear to be in the category of honoring an idol and symbolically ascribing powers to it. Otherwise, why throw money, which is clearly an act of beseeching a power for returned good fortune?

7. If something has been prepared to be offered to an idol, but has not yet been offered, it is permitted for personal use. One should be strict, however, and not use anything found in the house of idol worship. Therefore, one should never take candles from the place of idol worship.[16]

It is doubtful whether one should purchase or use sticks of incense sold by any of the idolatrous religions or pseudo-religions. For example, as most Hindu sects are pantheistic and idolatrous, incense and health foods

---

[16] Ibid.

purchased from such groups are questionable, for the foods themselves may have been worshiped.

In truth, any religious food discipline wherein the foods themselves or the combinations of the foods themselves are honored as miraculous in their health-giving properties[17] may be idolatrous.

Concerning the verse, *"Man does not live by bread alone, but by every word that proceeds from the mouth of God" (Deuteronomy 8:3),"* we are taught that it is not the bread itself which nurtures the body of man and gives it strength but the word of God, which is spiritually clothed within the bread and gives the bread its existence.[18]

Obviously, the same is true of any food or herb or wonder drug that heals, it is actually the power of God within that food or herb or wonder drug that is the healing agent.[19]

---

[17] Such as macrobiotic's reverence of whole grain brown rice.

[18] *Torah Or, Beshallach,* 65b, column 4

[19] Rebbe Nachman of Breslev taught that doctors demonstrate the great healing power of God. They show that God can heal a person even though the person places a doctor between himself and God.

8. If one offers excrement to an idol or pours a libation of urine for it, he transgresses, as this falls in the category of sprinkling [blood], one of the four services in the Holy Temple in Jerusalem.[20]

9. If someone slaughters an animal that is missing one of its limbs, he is held harmless unless this is the idol's particular service.

10. If a man lifts a brick and says to it, "You are my god," or any such similar speech, he is liable for idolatry. Even if he would retract immediately and say, "This is not my god," his retraction is of no help. This does not mean that the person cannot repent. He surely can repent and God will forgive his idolatry. But if there are witnesses who heard his speech, he will be brought to trial and condemned as an idolater notwithstanding his retraction or his repentance.

Repentance is good only between man and God. Jurists and courts of law lack the power to search a man's

---

[20] *Mishneh Torah,* Laws of Idolatry, 3:4

heart to determine the sincerity of his repentance. This only God can do.[21]

11. One who worships an idol according to its prescribed ritual is liable, even if he does it contemptuously. For example, if one defecates in front of Peor in order to disgrace the idol, since he performs the prescribed worship, he is liable.[22]

12. So long as a person accepts the idol as god, even if he worships it only because its workmanship is stunningly beautiful or because he superstitiously fears that some evil will otherwise befall him, he is liable.[23]

13. If a person serves an idol in the manner of one of the four forms of service used in the Holy Temple in Jerusalem – prostrating, sacrificing (including incense), sprinkling sacrificial blood, pouring drink offerings – and serves the idol with love and fear, but without accepting it as a god, he is held harmless.

---

[21] *Babylonian Talmud, Makkot* 13b, commentary of Rashi, "Rabbi Akiva says that you are cut off."

[22] *Mishneh Torah,* Laws of Idolatry, 3: 5

[23] Ibid., 3:6

If he hugs it or kisses it or dusts it off or pours water on it to cleanse the dust off it or anoints it or clothes it or does other things in order to honor it, these are in the category of prostrating oneself to it.

14. If a thorn gets stuck in a person's foot while he is in front of an idol, he should not bend down to remove it, as it appears he is bowing down to the idol. This holds true even if there is no one around to observe the act. This is also true if he drops his money in front of the idol and wishes to pick it up. Rather, the person should first sit, then remove the thorn or pick up the money.[24] Or he should turn his back to the idol or turn aside from it prior to removing the thorn or picking up the money. And if for any reason a person has to remove his hat for a personal need, he should not remove it until he passes before the idol so that it does not appear as if he is removing it to pay respects to the idol.

Note: There is a medieval house of idolatrous worship in Jerusalem that attracts many tourists. The door leading to the room where the idol is kept is extremely low so that

---

[24] Ibid., 3:7

anyone entering the room must bend down to enter, thus forcing each tourist who enters the room appear as if he or she were bowing to the idol.

15. If there is a fountain made with statuary that pour water from the mouth of the statue, a person should not drink from this water by placing his mouth to the statue's mouth as it would appear as if he is kissing it.[25]

16. One is forbidden to commission a craftsman to make an idol for himself even if he does not intend to serve it. Also it is forbidden to make an idol with one's own hands even if the idol is meant for someone else and the maker does not intend to serve it. All the more so, it is forbidden to make an idol with one's own hands for oneself.[26]

17. It is forbidden to make statuary for ornamental purposes, even though the figures are not idols; that is, one should not make images of gold or silver that are merely for artistic purposes because he might cause others to mistake them for idols.

---

[25] *Chochmat Adam,* Laws of Idolatry, 87:8

[26] *Mishneh Torah,* Laws of Idolatry, 23:9

This prohibition pertains to forms with human characteristics in three-dimensional relief. Though forbidden, such actions do not warrant capital punishment.[27]

18. An image that is concave rather than in relief, or two-dimensional such as paintings or woven tapestry, is permitted.

19. It is forbidden to wear a ring that has a seal on it in the image of a man (a cameo) if the image protrudes in relief, but it may be used as a seal.

If the image is concave, it may be worn, but it is forbidden to use it as a seal because the seal creates an image in relief.[28]

20. It is forbidden to form images of the sun or moon or stars or constellations or of the angels or a single form of the four faces of the Chariot[29] that Ezekiel saw, since it is forbidden to make images of the ministering angels that

---

[27] Ibid., 3:10
[28] Ibid., 3:11
[29] See the Book of Ezekiel 1:4-15.

serve God. Such figures may not even be made in two-dimensional form.

21. According to other opinions, it is forbidden to make forms of the angels and the chariot only in three-dimensional form. Drawing them on canvas or weaving these images on cloth or painting them on stone would be permitted since this form of expression is not three dimensional.[30]

However, even this latter lenient opinion forbids the drawing of the sun, moon, or stars in their complete form in a two-dimensional drawing because the sun and the moon appear to us two dimensionally in the sky.[31]

22. Concerning a sculpture of man, some authorities say the face by itself is forbidden. Others say that sculpture becomes forbidden only if the whole face is made with its body.

According to this second opinion, making a human body with its face is permitted as long as one does not make the complete body. However, it is proper to

---

[30] *Chochmat Adam,* Laws of Idolatry, 85:3

[31] Ibid., 85:5

follow the stricter opinion even if the sculpture is made just for beauty.[32]

23. It is not forbidden to keep or hold the image of a man in one's hand unless it is distinctly the image that which is worshiped as a god. Any other human image may be kept or held, so long as the image is slightly distorted or damaged, such as by chipping the nose, to dispel any suspicion of its being an idolatrous form. This act of damaging an image is called nullifying the idol.[33]

24. It is permitted to make statuary of trees and of wild or domestic animals, even of animals which are symbols in astrology, such as the lion, ram, or bull. One may make the full form of these figures and retain them in his possession. However, one may not make one form of all twelve astrological symbols.[34]

25. There is a stricter opinion forbidding all three-dimensional forms, whether they are in relief or

---

[32] Ibid., 85:4
[33] Ibid., 85:6
[34] Ibid., 85:7

concave. This opinion forbids making such forms in order to keep them in one's possession.[35]

26. One should never stare at three-dimensional images of idolatrous figures of man. Such gazing is spiritually damaging. But images upon a ring, since they are commonly found without idolatrous connotations, may be gazed upon.[36]

27. The three chief idolatrous images in the world are:

A. The dragon, which is a deification of the primordial serpent.[37]

B. A full figure of a man offering the beholder something (such as the globe of the world) from the palm of his hand.[38] This image is commonly found today in front of some Catholic Churches.[39]

C. A woman nursing an infant. This is an idolatrous perversion of Eve, the mother of all mankind. It became the symbol of the queen of heaven and is an

---

[35] Ibid., 85:8

[36] Ibid., 85:9

[37] Babylonian Talmud, Avodah Zara 42b

[38] Ibid., 41a

[39] *Shulchan Arukh, Yoreh Deah,* 141:1, *Shach* note 4

image that still pervades numerous cultures and religions.[40]

PART THREE: *Persuading others to serve an idol; false prophets.*

1. There is a difference of opinion whether the Children of Noah transgress the commandment of idolatry by persuading someone else to worship an idol. One opinion states that the Children of Noah do not transgress this commandment by leading others to serve an idol. The other opinion states that one is liable for the death penalty, but only if he leads a Jew away from the worship of the God of Israel and convinces him or her to serve an idol. If, however, one Noahide convinces another Noahide to serve an idol, he is not liable for punishment in a court of law, but since he has denied himself and the other person the opportunity of being close to God, he is punished from heaven.[41]

---

[40] *Chochmat Adam,* Laws of Idolatry, chapter *85,* law *2*

[41] S'dei Chemed, Peat HaSadeh, The Set Category Gimel, section 6, note 26

2. If a person says, "The idol said to me, 'Worship!' or he says, "God said to me, 'Worship the idol,' he is a false prophet. If he influences the majority of a city, he is stoned to death.[42]

3. A seducer to idol worship is equally liable whether he uses singular or plural expressions in his seduction. For example, if he says, "I will go and worship the idol," or, "Let us go and worship this idol," he is a seducer.

4. One who convinces others to worship him as an idol and says to them, "Serve me," and they worship him, he is stoned to death. If they accept him as their god but do not worship him, he is not stoned.[43]

5. If a prophet prophesies in the name of an idol and says something to the effect of, "This particular idol or this particular star said to me that it is an obligation to do such-and-such or not to do such-and-such," even if his

---

[42] Mishneh Torah, Laws of Idolatry, 5:2
[43] Ibid., 5:5

words teach the law correctly, he is subject to the death penalty for idolatry.[44]

6. It is forbidden to establish a law or to refute a law by the authority of someone who prophesies in the name of an idol. Nor do we ask him to produce a sign or a miracle. If he does so by his own volition, we pay no attention to it nor do we reflect about it. Anyone who thinks about these miracles and says, "Perhaps they are true," transgresses a law.[45]

Even if he were to walk on the water or raise the dead, we are to pay no attention to these acts. Such miracles are a test of our faith in God.

7. Similarly, a false prophet is killed by strangulation even if he prophesies in the name of God and teaches the Seven Universal Laws correctly, neither adding nor subtracting from their true meaning.

8. One who prophesies words that he did not hear in a prophetic vision or one who hears the words of a true prophet and says that they were received by him and not

---

[44] Ibid., 5:6

[45] Ibid., 5:7

the true prophet and he prophesies concerning these words, is a false prophet.[46]

9. One who holds himself back from killing a false prophet is a transgressor. And it matters not whether he fears to act because of the false prophet's exalted position, or because he is fearful of the false prophet's words.[47]

All false prophets, their disciples, and other idolatrous practitioners instill fear in the hearts of their victims, usually by threats of eternal damnation, hellfire, or other similar terrors. One can strengthen his heart against these threats by remembering that God is All Merciful and rewards and punishes according to a person's deeds, and that His punishments come as correction and purification of the soul. As King David wrote, *"Do not place your trust in benefactors, nor in the son of man in whom there is no salvation. Fortunate is he whose helper is the God of Jacob, whose hope rests upon the Lord his God" (Psalms 146:3,5).)*

---

[46] Ibid., 5:8
[47] Ibid., 5:9

10. A man should not use an idol or a house of idolatry as a signpost, such as telling his friend, "Meet me next to this particular house of idolatry."[48]

PART FOUR: *The idolatrous pillar; benefiting or profiting from idols.*

1. A pillar that serves as a central point of worship for gatherings of people is called a *matzeva,* a forbidden pillar. It is forbidden even if the people come to it in order to worship God, for this was the way of the ancient idolaters.[49]

Anyone who erects such a pillar performs a forbidden act, but is not executed for it.[50]

2. A stone floor with figures carved on it to attract the eye is called a figured stone and is forbidden. Even if one bows down on it with the intention of honoring God, he

---

[48] Ibid., 5:11

[49] The Kaaba stone in Mecca is just such a forbidden pillar. And the concept of the forbidden pillar is still with us today, at least conceptually. The film, Space Odyssey: 2001, was written as praise of the powers of an idolatrous pillar.

[50] Ibid., 6:6

performs a forbidden act, for this was the way of the idolater, but he is not executed for it. The way of idol worship was to lay a stone floor such as this before the idol. All stood on the figured stone floor, then bowed before the idol. Therefore, one should not employ a similar practice concerning the worship of God.

3. The previous law applies in all places but the Holy Temple in Jerusalem, where it is permissible to bow down to God upon a stone floor.[51]

4. One who bows down on a figured stone floor does not transgress unless he bows in total prostration, spreading his arms and legs. But if he bows to an actual idol, even if the figured stone was merely a floor placed before the idol, or whether he bows down in complete prostration or merely bows from the waist, he transgresses the prohibition against idolatry and is executed for it.[52]

5. It is a commandment to destroy all idols and everything used in serving them and anything made because of them. In the Land of Israel it is a commandment to pursue the

---

[51] Ibid., 6:7

[52] Ibid., 6:6

idol until it is destroyed and driven completely from the land.[53]

6. It is forbidden to derive pleasure or benefit from actual idols and all items needed for their service or sacrifices[54] and all that has been made to beautify them.[55] Anyone who benefits from any of these transgresses but is not executed for it.[56]

7. One is forbidden to benefit or use an animal that has been offered to an idol, including the animal's bones, horns, hooves, skin or excrement. Therefore, if there is a skin with a mark on it that indicates this skin was offered to an idol, such as a round hole torn opposite the heart of the animal, this skin is forbidden for use in any way.[57]

8. The difference between an idol belonging to a Noahide and the idol of an Israelite is that the former is forbidden immediately after its making is completed even though it

---

[53] Ibid., 7:1

[54] Such as wine or incense, etc.

[55] For instance, candles or curtains made to provide a beautiful environment to honor the idol.

[56] Ibid., 7:2

[57] Ibid., 7:3

has not yet been served. A Noahide's idol becomes a god from the moment it exists as a graven image. The idol of an Israelite is not forbidden until it is served.[58]

9. A Noahide who inherits an idol from his idolatrous father should cast it into the sea or dispose of it in some other definitive way.[59]

10. Figures and images that are made for artistic purposes and not idolatry are permitted for pleasure or profit. Those that appear to have been made for idolatry are forbidden. A full-figured statue that holds a staff or a bird or a globe or a sword or a crown and a ring in its hand is presumed to be an idol and it is forbidden for any use. These symbols all indicate rulership – the staff because he rules over the world, a bird because it flies above all and its eyes gaze down upon all, a ball because it represents the globe of the earth which he holds in his hand, and so forth. Otherwise, it is presumed to be of nothing more than artistic beauty and is permitted.[60]

---

[58] Ibid., 7:4
[59] Ibid., 7:5
[60] Ibid., 7:6

11. Crosses that are publicly displayed in Christian houses of worship are in the category of idols since people give honor to them, remove their hats before them, and bow down or genuflect to them.[61] However, the cross that hangs around a person's neck is considered a memorial and is permitted. Other personal uses like hanging a cross from the rear view mirror of an automobile are also permitted.[62]

12. However, priests who have crosses in their vestments or around their necks represent something very different from the cross of a person who wears it as a memorial, since the priest stands as a figure of religious authority. Therefore, one must never bow to such priests nor remove the hat in front of them nor do anything that may give the appearance that one worships the cross worn by a priest. If one bows or removes a hat as a gesture of giving honor to God, it must be discreetly away from the presence of such a cross, and preferably prior to the priest's appearance.

---

[61] All the more so, if the figure of Jesus is hanging from the cross.
[62] *Chochmat Adam*, Laws of Idolatry, chapter *85,* law 1

If it is in a place and a sect where it is known that these worshipers do not bow down to their images, but merely give honor to the priests that wear them, then one can be lenient to avoid offending these priests. But where it is known that the people do bow down to their statues and crosses in a manner that clearly appears idolatrous, one must be strict and avoid this.

13. One need not be strict about the wearing of a medal around the neck for luck when traveling or the like,[63] since the image on the medal is not worshiped.

14. If one finds vessels such as jewelry or expensive fabrics with images on them, if it is known that these images were made in the name of idol worship such as those found in India, they are certainly forbidden. But if one is not sure what the images were made for, or if they are found on non-precious vessels, such as simple vessels used for water or other foods, they are not forbidden.[64]

15. Today, people are not so attached to their idols, even to the images that they serve, such as the cross or a

---

[63] Like a St. Christopher's medal or a jade Buddha.

[64] Ibid., 85:2

nursing mother with her child. Because of this, if a vessel is found in Western lands, it can be assumed that the images are for beauty or a memorial and not for idolatry. Thus, the vessel would be permitted for use, but one is advised not to keep it his possession as it might convey the impression that the owner is an idolater.

16. It is idolatry to consume food or drink with the idea that it is the substance of a god and that the person consuming them is therefore assimilating the substance of the god into his own being.

Note: Historically, non-Jewish nations have fallen into idolatrous practices because of a lack of discernment between *Elohah* and *Elohut* – God and Godliness. One can say that all of creation is Godly because it all contains God's life force, but to say that anything of creation is God is idolatry.

17. It is forbidden to use vessels one finds, upon which appear the figure of a sun or a moon or a dragon if the vessel is of gold or silver. Similarly, if one finds a cloth

of silk with scarlet color with these images on them or rings or earrings with these images, they are forbidden.[65]

18. If one finds these images on other less precious articles, they are permissible because they are presumed to have been made for artistic purposes and are merely ornamental.

19. Idols and other articles used for their worship cause objects that they become mixed up with to be forbidden, even if the idolatrous articles are but a small factor in the number of objects.

For example: if an idol is mixed in with ornamental figures, even if the idol is but one in a thousand of the figures, everything is forbidden and must be thrown into the Dead Sea or similar water where metal will corrode or be lost.[66]

20. If a person finds money or vessels on the head of an idol, and the items appear to be placed there as an expression of contempt, they are permissible for use. For example: a purse found hanging on the neck of the idol, a

---

[65] *Mishneh Torah,* Laws of Idolatry, chapter 7, law 8

[66] Mishneh Torah, Laws of Idolatry, 7:9

cloth draped over its head, a vessel turned upside down and placed on top of its head – all these are permissible. These items were obviously placed there to disgrace the idol, and so it is with anything similar to this.[67] Conversely, if the objects appear to be there to honor the idol, they are forbidden.

21. If there is a garden or pool with an ornamental idol in it, one may use either the garden or the pool so long as it is not expressly for the benefit of the idol's priests. But if it is for the priests, it is forbidden for use.[68]

22. If the garden or pool is there for the idol and for the general populace, even if the priests use it as well, one may use it so long as no fee is paid.

23. It is forbidden to trade in a store from which profits are used for the upkeep of an idol. However, if the profits are collected by the government and they in turn support the upkeep of the idol, then it is permissible to trade in the store.[69]

---

[67] Ibid., 7:16

[68] Ibid., 7:17

[69] *Chochmat Adam,* Laws of Idolatry, chapter *86,* law *3*

24. If those engaged in the upkeep of idols collect taxes for the needs of the idols, it is forbidden to pay them any taxes. However, if the profits first go to the government, which in turn dispenses money for the upkeep of idols, it is permissible to pay the taxes.

25. Bread that is given to idolatrous priests is permissible because this bread is not offered to the idol but is the priests' portion.[70]

26. Wax candles that were lit before an idol for ornamentation are forbidden even after they were extinguished because the intention may have been to relight them. But if they were extinguished without the intention of relighting, they may be used. However, even if the candles were knowingly extinguished without the intention of relighting them, they may not be used in any way for the honor of God or to fulfill a commandment, such as to illuminate a house of worship or to have light to study the Torah.[71]

---

[70] Ibid., 84:9

[71] Ibid., 84:10

PART FIVE: *Things remaining permissible despite an involvement with idolatry; idolatrous trees; nullification of idols.*[72]

1. Anything that cannot be handled by man or made by man, even though it is worshiped, is permissible for use. Therefore, even if idolaters worship mountains or hills, trees that grow naturally or were planted for fruit, excluding those planted originally for idolatrous reasons, public streams or animals, all are permissible for use. And it is permissible to eat fruit that was worshiped so long as it remains in a state of natural growth, attached to the tree or bush, and it is permissible to eat worshiped animals that have not been sacrificed.

An animal that is designated for use in idolatry as an offering, prior to its being offered, may be used or eaten. But once the animal is used for the idol, even in the slightest way, it becomes forbidden.

---

[72] Basically, there are two kinds of forbidden idols. One is an object or image that represents the god and is worshipped as a form of representation, such as is the case in some branches of Christianity and Buddhism where people worship statues of Jesus or Buddha. The other is where the worshippers believe that the god has placed his essence within the idol itself, such as with the Hindu god Krishna and the ancient Philistine worship of Dagan.

For example, if the animal has been slaughtered for idolatry or has been exchanged for an idol or has been exchanged for something that has been exchanged for an idol, it is forbidden, as it now has monetarily equivalent to an idol.[73]

2. In the above situation, it is assumed that a person's own animal is used for idolatry; but when a person takes another's animal without permission and slaughters it for idolatry or exchanges it, it remains permissible for use. A person cannot cause anything to become forbidden which is not his own.

3. If one bows down to the earth in its natural state, the ground to which he bows does not become forbidden, but if he digs pits, ditches, or caves in the name of idolatry, the ground becomes forbidden.

4. If a person bows down to water which has been displaced from its natural state by a wave washing it into a ditch or the like, it is not forbidden water. But if he takes

---

[73] *Mishneh Torah*, Laws of Idolatry, 8:1

the water in his hand and bows down to it, it becomes forbidden.[74]

5. Rocks of a mountain that a person worships are permissible so long as they remain in their natural place, but if they are handled and moved, then worshiped, they become forbidden.

6. If a person erected a pillar or even set up a stone with the intention of worshiping it, but he did not worship it, then other idolaters came along and worshiped it, it is forbidden, as this is considered an idolatrous pillar.[75]

7. A tree planted in order that it may be worshiped as an idol is forbidden. Equally forbidden are its branches, fruit, shade and anything that might give one some kind of benefit. This tree is called an *asherah*, and is specifically mentioned in the Torah.[76]

---

[74] Ibid., 8:2

[75] Ibid., 8:3

[76] Deuteronomy 16:21.

8. If a tree is bowed to, although its trunk is permissible, all the shoots and fruit and branches and leaves that come forth during the time that it is worshiped are forbidden.

9. If idolaters watched the fruit of a tree and said that the fruit is there for them to make a drink for an idolatrous temple, and they made the drink and drank it on the day of their festival, this tree is forbidden. It is considered as if they planted it for idolatry in the first place and this is why its fruit was used.

10. If an idol stands underneath a tree, so long as it is there, the tree is forbidden. It is considered an accessory to idol worship and any pleasure from this tree, even its shade, is forbidden. If the idol is removed, the tree becomes permissible, for the tree itself was never served as an idol.[77]

11. If a house was not made or served as an idol, but was renovated, plastered, and decorated with images that were inlaid or carved in relief in the name of an idol, one should remove the renovations. They are forbidden because they

---

[77] Op. cit., 8:4

were made to serve an idol. Then the rest of the house is permissible for use.

12. If one brings idols into a house, for as long as they are in the house it forbidden for use, as it is considered an accessory to idol worship. Once the idols are removed in a way that indicates a nullification of the house's use as an accessory to them, the house becomes permissible. If the idols were brought there by an idolatrous Noahide, and an Israelite removes them from the house, this does not represent a nullification, because it may be construed that the Noahide wishes the idols to remain, but the Israelite did not. Therefore, just as a Noahide brought the idols into the house, a Noahide must take the idols out of the house in order for it to be considered a nullification of the house's status as an accessory to idol worship.[78]

13. One may not use a forbidden house in any way. One may not enter it or sit in its shade. However, it is permissible to pass through its shadow.[79]

---

[78] *Chochmat Adam,* Laws of Idolatry, *84:*15

[79] Ibid., 84:16

14. It is also advised that one should distance oneself at least eight feet from the entrance of a house of idol worship.

15. It is forbidden to listen to the music, smell the fragrance, or gaze at the ornaments of idol worship. Certainly, one is forbidden to gaze at the idol itself.

16. If one must walk near a place of idol worship, he should cover his eyes, stop up his ears, and hold his nose to avoid having sensory benefit from the idolatry.[80]

Even if the person has no intention of taking pleasure from these sights, sounds, and smells, he is should still conduct himself in the manner described, since he will certainly receive some pleasure from them if he does not so act.

17. If an idol rests on a stone, the stone is forbidden for use for as long as the idol is there. When it is removed, the stone is permissible for use.[81]

---

[80] It is common for idol worship, particularly in the orient, to burn incense and chant melodies.

[81] *Mishneh Torah,* Laws of Idolatry, chapter *8,* law *5*

18. If one has a house with a common wall to a house of idol worship and his house falls, he should not rebuild it as it was, but build it completely within his own property so that he shares no wall with the idolatrous house. The space that remains between his house and the house of idolatry he should fill with rubble so that the house of idolatry not be enlarged to encroach on his territory.

If he has a common wall with an idolatrous house, he should measure the thickness of the wall. The inner half of the wall is his and the outer half belongs to the idolatrous house. The stone or wood or dirt from the outer half is forbidden for any use.

19. The proper manner of destroying an idol and all the articles that are forbidden along with the idol is to grind them to powder and scatter them to the wind, or they should be burned and dumped into the Dead Sea or a similar body of water to corrode and be forever lost.[82]

20. An idolatrous figure is nullified by chipping off the tip of the nose or the tip of the ear or the tip of the finger or by hammering in a portion of its face even though no

---

[82] Ibid., 8:6

material is lost or by handing the figure over to a Jew who smelts metal. All these constitute nullification.[83]

Once nullified, the figure is permissible to own and use.[84]

21. An idol or any accessory to an idol, if it is nullified as an idol, becomes permissible for use. But anything that is offered up to the idol remains forbidden forever, and nullification is of no help.[85]

The general rule is that nullification must be performed by the one who worshiped the idol. If one who did not worship the idol nullifies it, the act accomplishes nothing.[86]

22. An idol worshiped by Jews can never be nullified, even if a Noahide owned it in partnership with a Jew. It is forbidden forever and must be destroyed. Similarly, if the idol of a Noahide comes into the possession of a Jew and

---

[83] Ibid., 8:10

[84] Ibid., 8:8

[85] *Chochmat Adam,* Laws of Idolatry; chapter 84, law 5

[86] *Mishneh Torah,* Laws of Idolatry, 8: 9

afterward the Noahide nullifies it, his nullification is of no help at all. It is forbidden forever.

23. An Israelite cannot nullify the idol of a Noahide, even if it is in the domain of the Noahide and the latter gave the Jew permission to nullify it. Only a Noahide can nullify his own idol.

24. A minor or a fool cannot nullify an idol.

25. The nullification of an idol automatically nullifies its accessories. But if the accessories themselves were nullified, although they are permissible for use, the idol itself remains prohibited.

26. Vessels that an idolatrous priest holds in his hand, such as a goblet, an incense tray, or a flute or other musical instrument, are considered accessories and require nullification.[87]

27. If an idolatrous figure is given as collateral or sold to a Noahide or to an Israelite who does not smelt it, or if it falls onto a garbage pile and it was not hauled away or it was stolen by robbers and was not recovered, or if one

---

[87] *Chochmat Adam,* Laws of Idolatry, 84:12

spat in front of it or urinated in front of it or dragged it on the ground or threw it into excrement, the idol is still prohibited as these do not constitute nullification.[88]

28. If the worshipers abandoned an idol and it is a time of peace, it is permissible for use as a nutcracker or a paperweight or the like, because it is considered nullified. Since the owners did not take it with them, it shows that they no longer value it. But if it is a time of war, it is forbidden because they may have abandoned it only because the war time situation caused them to flee without it.[89]

29. If an idol broke in half by itself[90] or by accident, the broken pieces are forbidden until they are nullified. Therefore, if one finds broken pieces of an idol, they are forbidden for use because it is possible its worshipers did not nullify it.

30. If the idol was made in pieces that fit together so that the average person could reassemble it, one has to nullify

---

[88] *Mishneh Torah,* Laws of Idolatry, 8:10

[89] Ibid., 8:11

[90] Such as by falling onto a pavement

each separate piece. If the idol cannot be reassembled, only one piece of it needs to be nullified.

31. An idol's altar that becomes damaged is still forbidden to use or to benefit from in any way, such as selling it, until the major portion of it has been damaged by the idolaters.[91]

PART SIX: *Ghosts and spirits; witchcraft; divination; astrology; charmers; necromancers*

1. One who consorts with ghosts or raises spirits to know hidden things or to know the future, and does it intentionally and of his own free will, is liable for idolatry.[92]

A Noahide is permanently warned about these matters.[93] Therefore, a claim of ignorance of the law is not an acceptable defense.

---

[91] Ibid., 8:12

[92] Ibid., 6:1

[93] This means that any person of normal intellect should realize that these things are evil and forbidden without having to be told.

2. If a person stands and burns incense and waves a myrtle branch in his hand and speaks whispered words to summon a spirit, then hears the summoned spirit speak to him, and if the spirit answers what it was asked in words that seem from below the earth in a deep voice that is not heard by the ear but felt in the thoughts; or if the practitioner takes the skull of a dead person and offers incense to it and uses arts of divination with whispers and various other rituals to the skull until he hears a low voice proceeding forth from under his armpit – all these acts come under the category of raising ghosts, and the practitioner is executed for doing them.

3. If a person places the bone of a certain bird or other kind of creature in his mouth and offers incense and performs other rituals until he falls to the ground like one stricken with an epileptic seizure, and if he speaks while in this trance things that will happen in the future, this is a form of idolatry and he is executed for it.[94]

---

[94] Ibid., 6:2

4. It is a matter of dispute whether a Noahide is forbidden to perform acts of witchcraft.[95]

If the final ruling of law is according to those who forbid it, the sorcerer or witch who is found guilty is given the penalty of death by stoning.[96]

Note: Inasmuch as such practices attach the practitioner to evil spiritual forces, they are harmful to his soul. People who claim that today there is no longer genuine witchcraft or genuine idolatry are ignorant and naive. Witchcraft as well as idol worship exist in the most complete and virulent meaning of the terms. Voodoo rites and satanic covens are flourishing today in England, the United States, Japan and throughout the rest of the world just as they did in ancient Egypt. We can even bear witness to a popular force in contemporary music where certain bands have declared themselves agents and disciples of Satan. Teenagers and adults by the millions have naively become enamored with these groups and their philosophies, which advocate sexual perversion and

---

[95] *Babylonian Talmud, Sanhedrin* 56b, commentary of the Meiri; *Mishneh Torah,* Laws of Idolatry, 11:4

[96] *Ibid.,* Raavad's commentary

physical cruelty. In effect, the fans of these rock groups are disciples of disciples of the satanic forces. Even though the dark side powers *"cannot do evil, neither is it in them to do good (Jeremiah 10:5),"* nevertheless one is well advised to avoid them, lest he give them power by acknowledging them. The protection against these evil rites and their intended results is to remember that evil as well as good comes solely from God, the Master of all forces, and He brings forth evil[97] in order to bestow free will to man so he can earn reward or punishment.

5. There is also a dispute concerning the permissibility of divination, the act of interpreting signs. Some authorities hold that it is forbidden and idolatrous, while others contend that it is permissible and even meritorious, approaching the level of prophecy, and that great and holy sages engaged in such practices.[98]

6. How does one engage in divination? For example, one might say, "Since my bread fell from my mouth or my staff fell from my hand, I will not go to a certain place today, because if I go today, my needs will not be done,"

---

[97] See Isaiah 45:7.

[98] *Kitzur Shulchan Arukh,* 166:2

or, "Since a fox passed on my right side, I will not go out of my house today, for if I do, a sneaky individual will meet me and trick me."[99]

7. Similarly, those who hear a bird calling and say, "It will be thus and it will not be thus," or, "It will be good to do such or it will not be good to do such," are engaging in divination.

8. Also, if a person proposes conditions, saying, "If thus and so happens to me, I will do thus and so, but if it does not happen to me, I will not do it," he is performing an act of divination.

9. Everything that is similar to the foregoing is divination. But even according to the opinion that considers it forbidden, divination is not punishable by the courts.

10. Certain interpretations of signs are considered permissible by all, however. It is not wrong to say, "This house that I built has been a sign of good luck from the moment I built it," or, "My wife has been a blessing, for from the moment I married her, I started becoming

---

[99] *Mishneh Torah,* Laws of Idolatry, 11:4

wealthy," or, "This animal that I acquired has brought me luck, for from the moment I got it, I started becoming wealthy."[100]

11. And similarly, if someone asks a child, "What verse did you learn?" if the child tells him something that indicates a blessing, and the person says, "This is a good sign," he does no wrong.

12. The difference of opinion occurs only when a person determines future actions by the interpretations of signs. A person who merely acknowledges a sign for something that already occurred is not practicing divination. There is another opinion that permits the interpreting of a sign to determine future action if the specific sign has proven successful three times in the past.

13. What is magic? It is engaging in exercises or disciplines that bring one to a euphoric state or that interrupt normal thought processes in order to proclaim future events. One might say, "Thus and so will happen

---

[100] Ibid., 11:5, Commentary of the Raavad

in the future or it will not happen," or he might say, "It is advisable to be careful of thus and so."[101]

14. There are those who engage in magic who use a stone or sand,[102] and there are those who bend down toward the earth and spin around and emit screams. There are those who look into a brass mirror or a crystal ball, then predict the future to one who is seeking this knowledge. There are those who lift a staff in their hands and lean on it and strike it until they alter their thought processes so as to be able to speak about the future.

Note: Today, many places abound with practitioners of these rites, which include horoscope predictions, palmistry, tarot cards, phrenology, and many other similar practices. These practitioners commonly establish businesses and advertise their services freely. To partake of such practices as a client is an act of faith in powers other than God's. What little gain might come from

---

[101] Ibid., 11:6.

[102] On August 23, 1999 in Central Park, the Dalai Lama drew a crowd of 40,000 people who watched him create a painting out of colored sand of "the four-faced god with twenty-four arms who subdues violence." He then poured the sand into a body of water where the sand's healing powers will sweep across the earth. This is witchcraft.

visiting such practitioners will certainly be more than offset by one's separation from God through involvement with these negative influences.

15. Moreover, the use of illusion to captivate the spectators by showing them things that are not in the natural order of things, and who makes it appear to the spectators that the illusionist did a miraculous deed, is in the category of magic. Such actions are forbidden as they lead to actual idolatrous practices.[103]

16. Although it is forbidden to practice magic or to consult one who practices magic, the courts do not punish for the practice of magic or for consulting a practitioner of magic.[104]

One must be reminded that all transgression outside the jurisdiction of the courts is punished by the hand of Heaven.

17. It is forbidden to be an astrological observer of the times. What is an observer of times? It is one who gives certain times that, according to astrology, indicate that

---

[103] Ibid., 11:9

[104] Ibid., 11:7

such a day is good and such a day is bad, such a day is proper to do thus and so and on such a day one should not do thus and so, or that a certain year or month is bad for certain acts such as marriage or engaging in a new career.[105]

18. Astrological forecasts are in a different category from using astrology to understand a person's characteristics and natural tendencies, the latter being a permissible practice.

19. Observing times is forbidden even if the observer of times does not perform any action but merely conveys falsehoods to gullible people and convinces them that these are words of truth and contain wisdom. All who conduct themselves and their activities because of astrological forecasts, working at a certain time or traveling at a certain time determined by the astrologers, transgress the law, but the courts do not punish for this.[106]

---

[105] Ibid., 11:8. Horoscope readings found in many daily newspapers are examples of this form of practice.

[106] Ibid., 11:9

20. What is a charmer? It is one who speaks words that are not of the language of people and that make no sense. None of the vulgar sounds or words or names spoken by the charmer contain the power to cause harm, nor do they do any good. But gullible people accept such things to the point where they will believe a charmer when he says, "If you are confronted by danger and will say thus and so, no harm can befall you." or, "If a person has thus and so said to him, he is protected from harm."[107]

21. The charmer might hold a key or a stone or any object while he says his nonsensical things. Anything similar to this is in the category of dealing in charms, and both the charmer and the one subjecting himself to the charmer transgress the law, but neither are punished by the courts.

22. If a person was bitten by a poisonous snake or stung by a scorpion, he is permitted to whisper any kind of spell he chooses over the place of the wound if he thinks it will help. This is allowed so the person, who is in mortal

---

[107] This is the Rambam's ruling. Others maintain that some similar practices are permissible, such as wearing a red or white string around one's wrist to protect from an evil eye or subduing a vicious dog by reciting the verse, "But against any of the Children of Israel no dog shall whet its tongue (Exodus 11:7)."

danger, can put his mind at ease and take courage. And even though what he says will certainly not help at all, since he is in danger he is allowed to do it to avoid panicking.[108]

23. One who whispers spells over another's wound or reads verses from the Torah over someone who is sick or dying, or similarly one who reads verses over a child to prevent the child from becoming fearful, is worse than one who is in the category of a diviner or a charmer, because by using the Holy Scriptures like this to cure the body, he denies the truth of the Torah, which comes as a cure for the soul.

But if one studies appropriate parts of the Torah or reads Psalms in order that the merit of reading them should protect him and save him from danger and harm, this is permissible.[109]

---

[108] Ibid.,, 11:11

[109] Ibid., 11:12. There is a practice prevalent today to randomly open a book written by a holy teacher in order to receive a blessing or get answers to questions. This is definitely divination. The Baal Shem Tov called such practices "treating the Torah like a game." He uses the same word (*keri*) as nocturnal emission or spilling one's seed.

It is certainly best to pray to God for protection and healing of every kind.

24. What is a necromancer? This is one who starves himself and sleeps overnight in a cemetery in order to bring the dead to him in a dream to inform him of something.[110]

25. There are also those who wear special kinds of clothing and speak incantations and offer incense and sleep alone in order to bring a specific dead person to come and speak to them in a dream.

26. In general, all who do various rites in order to summon the dead so as to learn information are in the category of necromancers and they transgress the law, but they are not punished by the courts for it.

27. It is forbidden to consult one who raises ghosts or spirits, because these practitioners are liable to the death penalty. One who consults with these practitioners but

---

[110] Ibid., 11:13

does not do the rituals himself is not punished by the courts.[111]

28. One who does not practice real witchcraft but merely uses sleight of hand or other illusions to fool onlookers transgresses the law but is not punished by the courts for it. It is, however, a serious matter, as such illusions are found in true witchcraft.[112]

Note: Witchcraft is definitely not a meaningless illusion. If it were, why would one performing it be subject to the death penalty? It is not unusual in our generation to find people who consider themselves "white witches," meaning that they do not use powers to perform any acts of evil or destruction, but use their knowledge to aid and benefit people. Nevertheless, the fact that they are dabbling in the use of "powers" places them squarely in the realm of serving forces other than G-d.

29. The foregoing are acts of deception and are false things, and through them the idolater deceives the people of the world in order to gain a following.

---

[111] Ibid., 11:14
[112] Ibid., 11:15

Without a single exception, the numerous cults, pseudo-religions, false messiahs, and demigods that are prevalent in the world today employ idolatrous practices to achieve spiritual power. Like the false prophets, they use spiritual threats to support their promises of salvation. Those who take refuge in these deceivers and find goodness in them should take warning: evil rarely announces itself as evil, otherwise people would avoid it.

Evil announces itself as good and mixes truth and goodness with its destructive falsehood. Herein lays its deceptive power. But those who are wise and possess true knowledge know by clear proof that these idolatrous practices are empty and without value. Those who are drawn to such things lack understanding and depart from the way of truth.[113]

Because of this, the Torah instructs everyone concerning these foolish vanities, *"Be wholehearted with the Lord your God (Deuteronomy 18:13)."* This means that people should put their trust in God Who took the Children of Israel out of the land of Egypt, and know that

---

[113] Ibid., 11:16

everything comes from Him and that He is good and the nature of good is to do good [114]

---

[114] Deut. 18:13, commentary of the Rashbam (Rabbi Samuel ben Meir)

Chapter Six

Blasphemy

PART ONE: *Definition of blasphemy.*

1. Blasphemy is the act of cursing the Creator. It is a deed so indescribably heinous that the Talmud, whenever referring to blasphemy, calls it by the euphemistic term "blessing God," to avoid directly expressing the idea of cursing God, the Father of all.

2. Blasphemy is the only means by which one transgresses the Seven Universal Commandments through the faculty of speech alone.

3. Blasphemy falls into the category of revenge. When someone is harmed by a person and seeks revenge, he may shout at the person or curse him. If the harm is great, the one seeking vengeance may not be satisfied by words alone but may physically strike out at the one who harmed him. In extreme cases, the vengeful person may not be satisfied until he kills. This is between a man and his neighbor. Between man and God it is somewhat different.

Man cannot kill God nor can he strike Him physically. The ultimate revenge that man can take against God is to curse Him. Therefore, blasphemy is seen as the expression of the desire to hurt God, even to erase His existence or murder Him.

4. The prohibition against blasphemy comes to teach us not to say anything evil against God nor to detract from His exaltedness in any way by intentionally using words to lessen the reverence and faith that are due Him.[1]

5. As with a transgression of any of the Seven Universal Commandments, before one can be tried in a court of law, there must be a witness to the deed who is willing to testify against the accused. This poses a problem, for how can the witness testify against the accused unless he repeats the blasphemous expression used, which would be a further transgression of this commandment?

6. In the Jewish courts of law, the matter is handled in the following manner. The witnesses during the entirety of the trial are directed to use a euphemistic phrase for the

---

[1] Sefer HaChinuch, Commandment 70

actual blasphemous utterance that they heard, eliminating reference to God in the phrase.[2]

Then, at the conclusion of the proceedings, the courtroom was cleared of all but those essential to the trial, and the witnesses were obliged to repeat the actual blasphemy that they heard. Upon hearing the blasphemy, the judges ripped their garments as one does for the death of a parent or any other tragedy that elicits grief.

7. Rabbi Hiyyah[3] declared that after the destruction of the Second Temple, one who heard blasphemy was no longer required to tear his garments, otherwise all would be walking around with their garments in tatters.[4]

8. The Code of Jewish Law, which is the prime authority in determining the religious obligations of the Israelite, states that a person who hears blasphemy is obligated to place the blasphemer under a ban of excommunication, regardless of whether the blasphemy was uttered against

---

[2] Mishnah Sanhedrin 7:5

[3] Hiyya bar Abba (180-230 CE), one of the early Amoraic sages and compiler of the Tosefta.

[4] Babylonian Talmud, Sanhedrin 60a

God's Name or any of His divine attributes,[5] whether in the Hebrew language or any of the other languages of the world, or whether the blasphemer was a Jew or a Gentile.[6] This ban of excommunication means that the person has no rights as a member of the community and that all are forbidden to speak to him.

9. Profaning the Lord of Hosts with one's lips, God forbid, is a transgression similar to but worse than idolatry. Whereas idolatry is the act of worshiping a created existence and thereby denying the true existence of the Creator, blasphemy is an acknowledgment of His existence but a denial of His greatness or His goodness. The blasphemer denies the truth that everything comes directly from God solely for mankind's benefit as a bestowal of goodness. Often the goodness is unrevealed as with a person's pain and suffering. At these times, one with a primitive consciousness or without a sufficient degree of faith in God can come to verbally express

---

[5] Such as *Rachum* (Merciful), *Chanun* (Gracious), etc.

[6] Shulchan Arukh, 340:37

dissatisfaction with his lot through blasphemy, and thus transgress the law.[7]

10. We see the essence of this problem in the Book of Job. God's faithful servant, Job, was struck by Satan with boils from the soles of his feet to the crown of his head. As he sat in agony from the affliction, his wife scolded him, saying, *"Are you still holding fast to your integrity? Blaspheme God and die." Job answered her, "You speak as one who is despicable. Should we accept only the good from God and not accept the evil?" Despite all this, Job did not sin with his lips (Job 2:9-10)."*

11. Consistent with this, it is a Jewish tradition to bless God for the bad as well as for the good.[8]

Even when, God forbid, one hears news of a person's death, he responds by saying, *Baruch Dayan Emet – Blessed be the True Judge.*[9]

12. Blasphemy as an expression of a deficient faith in God is characterized by the false notion that there are two

---

[7] Rambam, Sefer HaMitzvot, Negative Commandment 317

[8] Mishnah Berachot 9:5

[9] Ibid., 9:2; Shulchan Arukh, Orach Chaim, 222:2

powers and two kingdoms, God's and Satan's. All such theology denies that God is the Lord and Master of all.

13. The Book of Job shows clearly that God is the Ruler of Satan as well as of everyone and everything else, for when Satan wished to test Job, he first petitioned God for permission, whereby God sets definite boundaries for Satan, commanding him not to take Job's life, saying, *"Behold, he is in thy hand, but guard his life (Job 2:6)."*

14. The teaching in Christian theology that the evil force rebelled against the Lord and set up a separate kingdom is tantamount to blasphemy, for it denigrates the Creator and denies His infinite majesty and His mastery over all forces.

15. Some authorities state that false oaths or meaningless oaths whereby one invokes the Name of God are forbidden under the category of blasphemy.[10]

An example of a false oath would be for one to take an oath in God's Name that a tree is a rock, and a

---

[10] *Mishneh Torah,* Laws of Kings, 10:7; *Mishneh l'Melech,* "I saw…"

meaningless oath would be for one to swear in God's Name that a tree is a tree.[11]

PART TWO: *Transgressing the prohibition of blasphemy; piety.*

1. The prohibition of blasphemy is transgressed even if one uses another term for God, for example, an attribute or epithet such as the Merciful One, the Heavenly Father, or any other descriptive term. No matter how one curses God, and no matter in what language, the one who transgresses this commandment is subject to the death penalty by a court of law.[12]

2. If anyone acknowledges that a form of idol worship is true, even though he does not serve it, it is as if he reviles and blasphemes the mighty and exalted Name of God. Whether a person is an idolater or a blasphemer, it is the same in that both deny God.[13]

---

[11] *Jerusalem Talmud, Nazir, 9:*1; *Pnei Moshe,* "Israel should not delay…"

[12] Mishneh Torah, Laws of Kings, 9:3

[13] Ibid., Laws of Idolatry, 2:6

3. One who blasphemes and instantly retracts his words is nonetheless guilty if he blasphemed in front of witnesses. If he blasphemes in private and his words are heard by no one other than himself and his Creator, let him repent and God will forgive his transgression.[14]

4. One who curses God in the name of idolatry is subject to being attacked and killed by zealots, who are, in turn, held harmless by the law. One who is not a zealot, but rather seeks retaliation against a transgressor because of a desire for justice, must begin proceedings through due process of law against the accused.

Note: A zealot is one who serves God with a selfless, passionate love and is jealous for God's honor. Reacting to a desecration of God's Name, the zealot takes immediate action to stop the desecration. If one has to ponder the situation or ask the opinion of another person wiser than he in such matters, his hesitation or intellectual inquiry takes him out of the category of the zealot, and he is forbidden to take action. The scriptural source for the action of a zealot is seen in the heroics of Phineas, who

---

[14] Ibid., 2:9

stopped a plague among the Children of Israel when he slew a prince of the tribe of Simeon and the Midianite woman with whom he was having forbidden sexual relations.[15]

5. It should be the goal of every one of the Children of Noah to strive to do more than the minimum that the law requires, for this is the meaning of piety and one who takes on responsibility for fulfilling the Seven Laws of Noah is called *Chasidei Umot HaOlam* – one of the pious of the nations. Bearing this in mind, a person is well advised to withhold speaking evil about his fellow man as well as against his Creator, for in God's image was man created, and a person who reviles his fellow insults God as well.

If by words alone a person destroys a favorable view of someone in another's mind, this is considered like killing him. And it matters not whether the destructive words are true or false.

---

[15] Numbers 25:7,8

6. Striving to go beyond the letter of the law has no limit, for the commandments of God are as deep as the ocean and as wide as the sky.[16]

  Since everything in creation reflects the hand of the Creator, a truly pious person withholds himself from speaking negatively against anything. There are times, however, when it is appropriate and even mandatory to speak out against someone. For instance, when someone knows that a person is engaged in wicked pursuits and it appears that others will follow his lead, then it becomes a great kindness and even an obligation to speak in condemnation of the transgressor.[17] It should always be remembered that gossip, slander, and tale-bearing, even when the statements are true will stand in the way of an individual's spiritual and moral growth.[18]

---

[16] Job 11:9

[17] *Horev,* Rabbi S. R. Hirsch, chapter 90, notes 582-584

[18] *Ibid.,* chapter 53, notes 386-392

Chapter Seven

Murder

1. The commandment prohibiting murder is explicitly stated to Noah by God: *"Whoever sheds the blood of man, by man shall his blood be shed, for He made man in the image of God (Genesis 9:6)."*

2. A Noahide who kills a human being, even a baby in the womb of its mother, receives the death penalty. This means that one who strikes a pregnant woman, thereby killing the fetus, incurs the death penalty.[19]

    The act must have been done at least forty days after conception.[20] Before forty days, the act is in the category of destruction of man's seed. For this, a

---

[19] Mishneh Torah, Laws of Kings, 9:4. It follows then that one who performs an abortion is liable for capital punishment.

[20] *Shulchan Arukh, Yoreh Deah,* 305:23

transgressor is liable for punishment from heaven, but not by a court of law on earth.

3. Men and women have an equal responsibility to observe the prohibition against murder, and any act for which a man is held liable, a woman is equally held liable.[21]

4. If a person kills someone who is terminally ill or is falling from the top of a cliff or is certain to die momentarily for any other reason, he nevertheless transgresses the prohibition against murder and is liable for punishment by the courts.[22]

This ruling places the idea of mercy killing or euthanasia squarely in the category of murder.

5. If one pushes a person onto railway tracks and a train subsequently comes and kills him, or if one leaves a person in a situation where he will surely starve to death, although the action only indirectly causes the person's death, it is murder and the act is punishable by the courts.

---

[21] Babylonian Talmud, Sanhedrin, 57b
[22] Mishneh Torah, Laws of Kings, 9:4

6. If a person sees someone pursuing another for the obvious or suspected intent of committing murder or with the intent of causing the pursued to commit a sin,[23] and the observer is able to stop the pursuer by wounding him, but kills him instead, he transgresses this commandment and receives the death penalty.

If, however, a person himself is being pursued, he is free to take any action necessary to save his own life.[24]

7. Authorities disagree as to whether it is permissible for a Noahide to kill a fetus in order to save the life of the mother. But all agree that taking the mother's life to save the fetus is murder and punishable by the courts.[25]

---

[23] Such as rape.

[24] *Ibid.,* Laws of Wounds and Damages, 8:10; see commentary of *Mishneh l'Melech*

[25] Babylonian Talmud, Sanhedrin 59a; Tosefot, "There is nothing known…"

8. If a Noahide kills someone through a messenger, both the messenger and the person who sent him are liable for punishment as murderers.[26]

9. A person is commanded to allow himself to be killed rather than kill. This means that if people try to compel a person on pain of death to kill someone, he must not commit murder regardless of the consequences.[27]

10. Suicide is forbidden under the Seven Universal Laws.[28]

11. There is no place of legal refuge for a murderer. Any relative on the father's side of a murder victim who can legally inherit property of the deceased may designate himself a "blood avenger." If the murder was committed intentionally with malice aforethought, it is the blood

---

[26] *Bereshit Rabba,* chapter *34; Mishneh Torah,* Laws of Murder and Guarding the Soul, 2:2. This would include abortion. For a ruling dealing with extenuating circumstances that may permit abortion, an rabbinic authority should be consulted, for every situation is judged on its own merit and requires personal supervision.

[27] Mishneh Torah, Laws of Kings, 9:2

[28] Genesis 9:5; Rashi; Rabbi Abraham Ibn Ezra (1089-1164) disagrees and indicates that Genesis 9:5 has nothing to do with suicide.

avenger's obligation to see that the murderer is brought to trial.

12. If the killing was manslaughter – that is, if the killer acted unintentionally but negligently, and it is a matter of a *ger toshav*[29] killing another *ger toshav*, the killer flees to a designated city of refuge until his trial comes up. If the courts rule that he was guilty of killing, but did so unintentionally, he must return to the city of refuge and reside there until the High Priest of the Jews dies,[30] then he is free to return to his home. If he leaves the city of refuge prior to the death of the High Priest, the blood avenger may find him and kill him. The blood avenger is held harmless for killing the manslaughterer.

If a *ger toshav* kills an Israelite unintentionally but negligently, or if he kills another *ger toshav* because he thought that it was permissible,[31] he is liable for the death penalty.

---

[29] A resident stranger or proselyte at the gate. This is a Noahide who has taken upon himself the Seven Universal Commandments. This person is one of the Chasidei Umot HaOlam, the Pious Ones of the Nations.

[30] The death of the righteous is atones for the generation.

[31] This is considered equal to intentional murder.

If a Noahide who does not observe the Seven Universal Commandments kills another Noahide in a circumstance of manslaughter, he is subject to the death penalty and the city of refuge affords him no protection.

In a case where a blood avenger kills the manslaughterer, and the relative of the slain manslaughterer seeks revenge against the blood avenger and kills him, that relative is deemed a murderer and is prosecuted as such.[32]

13. There is a difference of opinion as to whether the Seven Universal Commandments include a commandment forbidding the willful destruction of a man's seed through masturbation or any other act of wasting semen.[33] All agree, however, that sexual relations with a woman who is incapable of bearing children is not considered wasting semen.

One opinion is that the commandment to be fruitful and multiply, having been given to Noah, but not

---

[32] *Mishneh Torah,* Laws of Kings, 10:1; Laws of Murder and Guarding the Soul, 5:3,

[33] *Shulchan Arukh, Even HaEzer,* 23:5, Rabbi Moses Isserles, the Rama

repeated to Moses, was in force only during those generations before the historical event of Mount Sinai. In those early times, wasting semen was considered among the most heinous of sins and a chief reason that God brought the Flood to destroy the world. The Torah clearly states that Judah's two sons, Er and Onan, were slain by God because *"the thing which he [Onan] did was evil in the eyes of the Lord (Genesis 38:10)."* However, this event took place prior to the giving of the Torah on Mount Sinai. This opinion concludes that since the commandment against wasting seed was not repeated by Moses at Mount Sinai, it was no longer in effect as part of the Seven Universal Commandments.[34]

The other opinion states that despite the fact that it was not repeated at Mount Sinai, since it was originally included in the Seven Universal Commandments, a man is forbidden to willfully destroy his seed, though the act is not punishable by the courts.

---

[34] *Babylonian Talmud, Sanhedrin* 59b, *Tosefot,* "Behold, be fruitful and multiply."

After a man has fulfilled his basic obligation of bringing a son and a daughter into the world, if he wishes then to use contraceptive devices, he should use a type that does not act directly on the semen. According to this viewpoint, masturbation is strictly forbidden.

In spiritual terms, the reason for the great concern and strictness concerning the wasting of a man's seed is that it is considered the willful destruction of his life-giving force and equated with life itself. Therefore, the destruction of a man's seed is related closely to murder, and even more, to the murder of one's own children.

Chapter Eight

Forbidden Sexual Relations

1. It is written, *"Therefore a man shall leave his father and his mother and shall cling to his wife and they shall be one flesh (Genesis 2:24)."*

According to the Holy Spirit this verse comes to instruct mankind concerning forbidden sexual relationships.[1]

The phrase, *"Therefore a man shall leave his father and his mother,"* forbids a man to have sexual relations with the wife of his father[2] even after the death of his father, when she is no longer considered a married woman. Obviously, this also includes his natural mother. The phrase, *"cling to his wife,"* comes to teach us that he shall have relations with his own wife and not another man's wife. *"To his wife"* comes to teach us that he shall have relations with the opposite gender, not with a male.

---

[1] Genesis 2:24, commentary of Rashi

[2] A woman his father married, but who is not his mother.

"And they shall be of one flesh" comes to exclude any animal, for an animal is not of one flesh with a man.[3]

2. A Noahide is forbidden to have relationships with certain relatives and with others to whom he or she is not related by blood. These are:

    A. Mother, even if his birth was the result of her having been seduced or raped.

    B. Father

    C. Daughter

    D. Father's sister

    E. Mother's sister[4]

3. Under the Seven Universal Commandments, one is permitted to have relations with individuals related through marriage after the death of the relative. According to some opinions,[5] this even includes a man's father's wife (not one's mother) after his father dies. Those falling in this category are:

    A. Father's wife who is not one's mother.

---

[3] Mishneh Torah, Laws of Kings, 9:5

[4] Babylonian Talmud, Sanhedrin 58a

[5] This opinion disagrees with what was stated above in reference to a father's wife who is not his mother.

    B. Brother's wife.

    C. Wife's sister.

    D. Daughter-in-law.

    E. Stepdaughter.

4. The opinion forbidding the father's wife after the death of the father is thought to include women that the father merely had sexual relations with, even if they were seduced or raped by the father.[6]

    Other authorities permit relations with the father's wife after his death, but forbid relations with either the father's or the mother's maternal sister.

5. It is argued in the name of Rabbi Akiva that all relationships that warrant the death penalty in a Jewish court of law also will receive the death penalty in a Noahide court of law. This includes relationships that exist through marriage.[7] The reason is that since one's father's wife is forbidden, others related through marriage, such as a

---

[6] Mishneh Torah, Laws of Kings, 9:6

[7] Such as a mother-in-law or a daughter-in-law.

mother-in-law, is forbidden. Such relationships are punishable by the courts.[8]

Other authorities say that only the father's wife is in this forbidden category, and they exclude others related through marriage.[9]

6. Forbidden sexual relationships with persons who are not relatives are:

A. A man with another man's wife.

B. A male with a male.

C. A person (male or female) with an animal.[10]

7. A Noahide man is forbidden to have relations with another man's wife, whether she is the wife of another Noahide or the wife of an Israelite.[11]

Although a Jewish man is forbidden to marry a Noahide woman and from the perspective of the Jewish man there is no marriage, nevertheless, the bond of

---

[8] Babylonian Talmud, Sanhedrin, 58b

[9] Ibid., Yebamot 98a, commentary of Ramban

[10] Mishneh Torah, Laws of Kings, 9:6. Female sheep and goats with Arab shepherds were rejected as offerings in the Holy Temple since it was presumed the shepherd had sexual contact with his animals.

[11] Babylonian Talmud, Sanhedrin 57b

marriage exists for her and she is forbidden to other men. Under the Seven Universal Commandments, a woman is considered to be a man's wife when the couple has sexual relations with the intention of consummating marriage.[12]

8. A man is not punished by the courts for having relations with a married woman unless he has sexual intercourse with her in the normal manner of vaginal penetration. Since this is considered to be the way for a man to be with a woman.[13]

But with other forbidden relationships, a man is liable for punishment for sodomy or any other complete sexual act. It does not have to be the normal way of intercourse.[14]

9. A man is liable for punishment even if there was only slight penetration during the act of intercourse.[15] Some

---

[12] *Mishneh Torah.* Laws of Women, 1:1, commentary of the *Maggid Mishneh*

[13] Ibid., Laws of Kings, 9:7

[14] Ibid., commentary of the Maggid Mishneh

[15] *Jerusalem Talmud, Kiddushin,* 1:1

opinions maintain that one is not liable for only slight penetration.[16]

10. A man is not punished by the courts for having relations with a married woman until she has consummated marriage with her husband. If she is engaged and not yet married, even if she is standing under the wedding canopy, and there has been no consummation of the marriage, the perpetrator is not liable for punishment by the courts. This legal ruling is in reference to a Noahide man with a Noahide woman. Regarding a Noahide man and an Israelite woman, whether she has consummated the marriage or is engaged but has not yet consummated the marriage, or she is married but has not consummated the marriage, he is liable for capital punishment.[17]

11. In times of slavery, if a Noahide man designated a specific female slave for his male slave and then had relations with her, he was killed because of it because she was considered another man's wife. However, the master was not condemned until it had become public knowledge

---

[16] Beit HaBechirah on Sanhedrin, p. 227

[17] Mishneh Torah, Laws of Kings, 9:7

that those particular slaves had been given to each other. When did she become permissible again? When she separated from the designated male slave and uncovered her head in the marketplace.[18]

12. The concept of divorce with regard to Noahides is a matter of dispute. One opinion holds that no divorce is possible.[19]

Another legal ruling states that no writ of divorce is necessary, rather that divorce is dependent solely on the volition of either spouse, even if the other one is against the divorce. They separate due to the desire of either party and the matter is concluded.[20]

Others contend that the woman may divorce her husband, but that the husband may not divorce his wife.[21]

13. One who caresses a forbidden member of the opposite sex, or hugs or kisses in a manner of lust, or has close

---

[18] This means she made it known publicly that she was available to another man. Ibid., 9:7

[19] *Babylonian Talmud, Sanhedrin* 58b, commentary of Rabbeinu Nissim

[20] Mishneh Torah, Laws of Kings, 9:8

[21] *Bereshit Rabba,* chapter 18, opinion of Rebbe Yochanan

personal contact for the sake of pleasure, transgresses the commandment prohibiting forbidden relationships, but is not punished by the courts.

In all cases where the courts are not empowered to act, punishment is delivered by God.[22]

14. It is forbidden to signal with the hands or the feet or to wink at any person who is in the category of a forbidden relationship. This includes any form of serious flirtation. One should not be frivolous or light-headed with anyone who is in a forbidden category, nor should a man deliberately smell the perfume or gaze at the beauty of a woman who is forbidden to him.[23]

15. A man is guilty of transgressing the commandment of forbidden sexual relations by having homosexual relations whether the other male is an adult or a child, whether the other male is consenting, coerced or forced, in public or in the privacy of one's own domicile.[24]

---

[22] *Mishneh Torah,* Laws of Forbidden Relationships, chapter 21, law 1

[23] Ibid., 21:2

[24] Ibid., Laws of Kings, 9:6

Note: In the Holy Scriptures, of all the forbidden sexual relationships mentioned, only homosexuality is described as an *"abomination to God."* Even bestiality is not so described. From a spiritual perspective, homosexuality is devastating, destroying both the body and the soul of those who engage in it. No homosexual was ever born into this world through a homosexual relationship. And although it is true that a person may have congenital tendencies towards homosexuality, it is like the child with the trait of throwing temper tantrums or banging its head against the wall. If the tendency is destructive, the goal is to seek correction. When a person is sick, the goal is to heal him.

Ultimately, homosexuals themselves will complain against those who misled them by condoning their practices and encouraging them, including politicians who pander to them as a constituency. In the end they will see that this deviation brings one to abnormal weakness and to horrible diseases as society has already discovered.[25]

---

[25] *Rights or Ills,* adapted from the works of the Lubavitcher Rebbe

In the context of history, every society that encouraged or condoned homosexuality was short-lived, terminated even at the height of its glory. Most notable of these was ancient Greece, which ruled the world and then was summarily voided in its prime. Ironically, it was the tiny Jewish nation led by the priestly Maccabees that broke the back of the mighty Greek Empire. It is no wonder that religious Jews are so outraged at contemporary society's permissive attitude towards homosexuality, which was the essence of western civilization's corrupt Hellenist legacy.

16. Though it violates the spirit of the Seven Universal Commandments, lesbianism is not explicitly stated as one of the forbidden relationships. Lesbianism is, however, deemed an immoral and unnatural relationship that destroys the order of the world. The Rambam forbids it as one of the evils of Egypt.

Prostitution is in the same general category; that is, while not strictly forbidden, it is deemed severely immoral and therefore violates the spirit of the Seven Universal Commandments.

17. Sexual relations with an animal are forbidden at any stage of the animal's maturity, even the day of its birth. A Noahide who has sexual relations with an animal is liable for punishment, but the animal is not killed.

In the case of a Jew copulating with an animal, both the person and the animal are killed.

18. The Children of Noah are considered related only through the mother. Those on the father's side are not considered relatives.[26]

This means that a man's half-sister of the same father but a different mother is not considered related to him and is permissible to him.[27]

19. There is an argument in the Talmud as to whether a Noahide is permitted to have a relationship with his daughter inasmuch as she is not considered his relative.[28]

---

[26] *Babylonian Talmud, Yebamot* 98a, commentary of Rashi, "Behold, the rabbis say…"

[27] *Mishneh Torah,* Laws of Forbidden Relationships, 14:10

[28] *Babylonian Talmud, Sanhedrin* 58b, commentary of the Ramban. If she is permitted to him, then Lot's sexual relations with his daughters were permissible acts.

The conclusion is that, despite the fact that his daughter is not considered his relative, she is nonetheless forbidden because she is in the same category as his mother, a parent-child relationship, and his mother is forbidden.[29]

20. In a homosexual or bestial act, one is liable even if there is only partial penetration.[30]

21. It is forbidden under the Seven Universal Commandments to castrate any male, whether man or animal or fowl.

In one opinion, castration of oneself is a transgression, but it is questionable whether it is forbidden to fulfill someone's request to castrate him or to agree to castrate his animal, despite its clearly being an act of maiming one of God's creatures. Nevertheless, even with so bizarre and irreversible an act as castration, repentance and forgiveness are possible through God's great mercy, as it is written, *"For thus has said the Lord concerning the eunuchs that keep My Sabbaths and*

---

[29] Ibid., commentary of *Beit HaBechirah*

[30] *Jerusalem Talmud, Kiddushin,* 1:1 and commentaries

choose that which pleases Me, and take hold of My covenant. I will give to them within My house and within My walls a place and a name better than sons and daughters; and an everlasting name will I give them that will not be cut off (Isaiah 56:4-5)."

Chapter Nine

Theft

1. Of all the categories of the Seven Laws of Noah, the prohibition against theft may be the most difficult to obey.

Human history and psychology are in clear agreement with the Talmudic statement, that "Man's soul has a craving and longing for incest and robbery."[1] But unlike incest, committing theft is often a simple matter in which the opportunity presents itself almost constantly. Moreover, the commandment prohibiting theft includes aspects that without careful Torah study might elude a person and be considered acceptable behavior. Therefore, a frequent review of the laws of theft is important.

2. The commandment prohibiting theft that was given to the Children of Noah is a single comprehensive law with many parts and details. It is virtually identical to the sixteen separate commandments dealing with theft that were given to the Children of Israel. This means that

---

[1] *Babylonian Talmud, Makkot* 23b

God's will concerning theft is essentially the same whether the person involved is an Israelite or a Noahide.[2] The only difference involves the return of a stolen object worth less than a pruta,[3] the smallest coin denomination in the times of the Talmud.[4] If such an object is stolen from an Israelite, it need not be returned, for the Israelite is presumed to forgive the theft of so small an object and forego its return; but the Noahide does not forego an object worth less than a pruta, and such a stolen object must therefore be returned to him.[5]

3. The commandment prohibiting theft holds men and women equally liable in every aspect and detail.[6]

---

[2] Armed robbery (*hamas* in Hebrew) was the sin that sealed the fate of mankind to bring the Great Flood in the generation of Noah. See Genesis 6:13.

[3] *Mishneh Torah,* Laws of Kings, 9:9

[4] Just as a frame of reference, a pruta might be compared to a one agora coin in Israeli money, which in 2013 would be worth one-third of a U.S. penny. Israel stopped minting the one agora coin in 1991. Today, the smallest denomination coin being minted in Israel is a ten agorot coin, worth about three U.S. pennies.

[5] *Babylonian Talmud, Sanhedrin* 57a

[6] *Encyclopedia Talmudica,* The Children of Noah, volume 3, page 348

4. One is liable for punishment whether he brazenly robs in public or sneaks into a house on a moonless night.[7]

5. One is liable to punishment by a court of law whether he steals money or any object or kidnaps a person. And he is liable no matter from whom he steals.

6. A Noahide who steals a beautiful woman from the enemy during time of war is liable for punishment. It is presumed that he kidnapped her and that she is a married woman.[8]

7. The Children of Noah are forbidden to engage in wars of land conquest, but if such a war does occur, and in the process a land is conquered, what the Noahide acquires of this new land belongs to him ex post facto.

8. Later authorities rule that a man who rapes or seduces a woman who is not forbidden to him is liable for punishment because he is stealing from the woman's worth for his own personal use.[9]

---

[7] *Mishneh Torah,* Laws of Kings, 9:9

[8] *Babylonian Talmud, Sanhedrin* 57b

[9] *Minhat Hinnukh,* Commandment 35

This judgment applies only to a man who seduces a woman, not to a woman who seduces a man. A woman is considered unable to truly seduce or rape a man, as a man must have an erection to have intercourse and therefore his involvement in the act is one of acceptance and volition.

9. The early Sages of Israel were in disagreement as to whether the Children of Noah were forbidden concerning usury and overpricing before the giving of the Torah.[10] In either case, both of these commandments are in effect today because they were given to Moses at Mount Sinai, not because God commanded Noah to follow them. It is a general principle of the Seven Universal Commandments that they are binding only because they were given on Mount Sinai. The great Jewish sage Nachmanides[11] states that overcharging is clearly one of the tenets of the commandment prohibiting theft.[12]

---

[10] *Babylonian Talmud, Baba Metzia 70b, Tosefot, "What is this, usury?"*

[11] *Rabbi Moses ben Nachman (1194-1270), known as the Ramban.*

[12] *Genesis 34:13, commentary of Ramban*

This means that a transaction whereby one is greatly overcharged is considered an illegal transaction and may be voided. Usury, the act of lending money at unfair interest rates, is in the same category. Usury is forbidden as an illegal transaction.

10. The category of overcharging includes the admonition against using false weights and measures. This applies to any storeowner or salesperson, whether he is selling fish or precious stones, or measuring land for sale, as it is written, *"You shall do no unrighteousness in judgment, in measuring land, in weight, or in measuring liquids (Leviticus 19:35)."*

Inasmuch as the act of falsely weighing and measuring is forbidden, it is similarly forbidden to have such false weights or measuring devices in one's possession, as it is written, *"You shall not have in your bag diverse weights, a great and a small (Deuteronomy 25:13)."*

Since sustenance comes from the hand of God, a man should earn it through honesty, not trickery. In Talmudic times, the fair amount of profit gained was thought to be one-sixth,[13] but since profit margins are considered somewhat relative and subjective, the fair amount remains to be determined by the norms set in each generation.

12. A Noahide is not obligated to return an object that he stole. But since he stole it, he is held accountable for the prescribed punishment in a court of law. This is according to Rashi's opinion, which holds that when a single act warrants two punishments, the stricter punishment is enforced and the lesser one is dropped. Other authorities argue that this principle applies only to an Israelite and the laws of the Torah, and that when a Noahide has stolen, he is obligated to return the stolen article to its rightful owner, despite the fact that he may have incurred the death penalty.[14]

13. One may well ask why the thief, who is going to be executed anyway,[15] should bother to return the stolen

---

[13] *Mishnah Baba Metzia,* 4:3

[14] *Babylonian Talmud, Avodah Zarah* 71b, *Tosefot,* "The Sons of Noah are..."

[15] See Chapter 11, Courts of Law, for a discussion as to whether violation of the commandment of theft earns the death penalty.

object. He could just as well leave it to his spouse or child or a friend and therefore have some indirect benefit.

The explanation goes right to the heart of the intent of God's Law, which is just and merciful at the same time. Every punishment meted out through the justice of the Noahide courts serves as an atonement, sparing the transgressor punishment in the Eternal World. This, of course, assumes that the convicted criminal repents for his transgression and returns to God before he is executed.

Because of the justice of the courts, therefore, a man can transgress and still repent and receive a share of the World to Come as a righteous person.

14. What happens then, if a man commits a crime and is not punished by the courts? Suppose there are two men, one who killed negligently but without premeditation and another who killed with malice aforethought. There were no witnesses to either crime. God will bring the two men together through Divine Providence. For instance, on a crowded street, the one who killed unintentionally might be driving a car, while the killer is crossing the street as a pedestrian. Not paying attention to what he is doing, the

driver runs through a stop sign, killing the pedestrian. So what has God wrought? The murderer is killed, and the manslaughterer is now held as a manslaughterer.[16]

15. A Noahide who strikes another Noahide transgresses the commandment against theft and is liable for punishment by the courts, for the damage he caused brought a physical and psychological loss to the person struck.[17] A Noahide who strikes an Israelite also violates the commandment of *kedushat Yisrael,* violating the sanctity of an Israelite.[18]

16. A person is forbidden to covet the property and physical dwelling place of another as expressed by the scriptural verse, *"You shall not covet your neighbor's house; you shall not covet your neighbor's wife, nor his manservant nor his maidservant nor his ox nor his ass nor anything that is your neighbor's (Exodus 20:14)."*[19]

---

[16] Exodus 21:13, commentary of Rashi, "But God caused it to come to hand…"

[17] Genesis 34:13, commentary of Ramban; *Encyclopedia Talmudica,* The Children of Noah, volume 3, page 257

[18] *Mishneh Torah,* Laws of Kings, 10:6

[19] *The Seven Laws of Noah,* Lichtenstein, page 22. The term covet is used twice, the first relates to some action taken to acquire an

17. Since the Children of Noah are commanded to withhold themselves from committing theft, they are similarly commanded concerning deterrents to that transgression, namely desire.[20]

Coveting something that belongs to another is in precisely the same category as desiring the object except it takes it a step further, involving action. Whereas desire remains something of the heart, total covetousness presupposes that the person does something to fulfill his desire, such as pressure the owner or plead with the owner to sell him his house or field.[21]

18. When mankind is judged each year on Rosh Hashanah, the first day of the Hebrew month of Tishrei, God apportions each person's income and sustenance and all forms of material acquisitions for the coming year. Nothing a person will do can add to what he has been allotted, and no one can take away what has been given to someone, as King Solomon wrote, *"The blessing of the*

---

object, the second relates to a desire for acquisition in the heart. The latter is obviously not punishable in a court of law because only God can know what is in a man's heart.

[20] *Sefer HaHinnukh,* Commandment 424

[21] *The Seven Laws of Noah,* Lichtenstein, page 24

Lord is that which makes rich, and painful labor adds nothing to it (Proverbs 10:22)*. Therefore, to desire what belongs to another, and all the more so to covet it, is an act that betrays a lack of faith in God, for it is said, *"Who is happy? One who is satisfied with his portion."*[22]

19. One is forbidden to enter another's property stealthily and take back one's own object, for thereby he is acting in the manner of a thief. Instead, one should confront the other and say, "This belongs to me, I am taking it."[23]

20. One is forbidden to add to one's own property by surreptitiously moving the landmarks back into the neighbor's property, as it is written, *"You shall not remove your neighbor's landmark (Deuteronomy 19:14)."*

21. This act of usurping one's land through moving a landmark involves the idea of unfair competition. For example, if a person has a business in an area that will only support one business of that type, and someone moves in across the street and opens the same kind of

---

[22] *Chapters of the Fathers, 4:1.*

[23] *Babylonian Talmud, Baba Kamma* 27b

business, this is said to be removing one's neighbor's landmark.[24] Or today, the prevalent act of duplicating books or films or recorded songs without permission, even for one's private use, is an act of moving your neighbor's landmark, for one who does this denies his neighbor the right to make a living.

22. It is forbidden to withhold the salary of a worker. If one hires a worker, it is incumbent on the employer to pay the worker his wages at the conclusion of the day's work, unless a different arrangement had been agreed upon ahead of time.[25]

It is similarly forbidden to refuse to repay a loan of money when one has the means to repay, or to refuse to return a borrowed object.[26]

All these are enjoined by the verse, *"You shall not oppress your neighbor, nor rob him (Leviticus 19:13)."*

Shulchan Arukh, Choshen Mishpat, 156:1-7

[24] *Deuteronomy 19:14.*

[25] *Mishneh Torah,* Laws of Kings, 9:9

[26] Genesis 34:13, commentary of the Ramban.

23. An employer who works in a field or in a restaurant is permitted to eat the produce of the field or some of the restaurant's food as he works if it is in connection with his work. For instance, if a person harvests grapes, he is permitted to snack on the grapes as he works. Similarly, if he is a cook, he is permitted to eat some of the restaurant's food. But, if he merely irrigates the land on which grapes grow, his snacking on grapes is considered theft. Similarly, if he is a dishwasher in a restaurant, his snacking on the restaurant's food is considered theft unless the owner expressly permits it. Even in permissible cases, the employee may snack only as he works. If he loads up a basket and secretly takes the food home to feed himself or his family, it is theft.[27]

24. If a person steals anything worth more than a *pruta* and then another steals it from him, both transgress the commandment prohibiting theft.

---

[27] *Mishneh Torah,* Laws of Kings, 9:9

Chapter Ten

The Limb of a Living Animal

1. There is some discussion as to whether or not the prohibition of eating the limb of a living animal was originally given to Adam, the first man. One opinion states that it was included in the original commandment forbidding the eating of the fruit of the tree of knowledge of good and evil.[1] According to this opinion, Adam, who was clearly given vegetation for food, as it is written, "And God said, Behold I have given you every herb bearing seed which is upon the face of the whole earth, and every tree upon which there is fruit of a tree bearing seed, to you these shall be for food" (Gen. 1:29), was not forbidden to eat meat, but was merely forbidden to kill animals for food. If the animal had died of itself, it was permissible as food.[2] What Noah was given, therefore, was permission to kill animals for food, but he was forbidden by God to eat the flesh of any animal while the

---

[1] Babylonian Talmud, Sanhedrin 56b

[2] Ibid., Tosefos, "He should eat…"

animal was still alive.³ According to the other opinion, Adam had received six of the Seven Universal Commandments and had been forbidden to eat the flesh of an animal in any manner. Only after the Flood was the leniency of permitting animal flesh instituted.⁴

This commandment is explicit, as it is written, "Every moving thing that lives shall be for you for food; just as the green herbs, I have given you everything. But flesh with its living soul, its blood, you shall not eat" (Gen.9:3-4). This does not mean that an animal's blood is its soul and God was forbidding man to drink animal blood. The vitalizing animal soul is contained within the blood, and this is what the commandment refers to, for when an animal dies, this vitalizing soul departs. So long as this vitalizing soul remains within the animal, its flesh is forbidden to man as food.⁵

At first glance, this commandment seems peculiarly out of place as one of the Seven Universal Commandments. How can eating the limb of a living

---

[3] Gen. 9:4, Rashi, "But flesh with the life…"
[4] Mishneh Torah, Laws of Kings, 9:1
[5] Lev. 17:14, Rashi; Gen. 9:4, S.R. Hirsch

animal take its place side by side with such monumental principles of human morality as those prohibiting idolatry or murder? Besides a few scattered sociological perversions in Africa and China, one is hard put to imagine who would even consider eating an animal's meat while the animal lives.

And yet this is precisely why this commandment may well epitomize the spirit of the Noahide Laws.[6] Although mankind is enjoined to obey these commandments as they appear, nevertheless the letter of the law serves only as a minimum, a starting point, which guarantees God's favor and ensures human morality. But, if man wishes to realize his spiritual greatness, he must tap into the infinite potential of the Seven Laws, using them to refine and elevate himself.

We see here that eating the limb of a living animal serves as a hint to the potential refinement that man can attain through his eating habits and by practicing kindness to God's creatures. For what man ingests as food is absorbed in his bloodstream and in every cell of his

---

[6] The Seven Laws of Noah, Lichtenstein, p. 56

body and thereby becomes part of his essential being. The person who eats snakes and monkeys will surely be different from the one who eats nuts and berries. And the mystical teachings state that the Holy Spirit will never rest on one who kills any creature, even the lowliest insect, purposelessly.[7]

2. The early Sages differ concerning the act of consuming the blood of an animal.[8] The Sages say that the Children of Noah contend that they were never forbidden blood as food.[9]

3. The Noahide may eat the flesh of an animal that dies by itself,[10] but there is an opinion stating that only the flesh of an animal killed through slaughtering is permissible.[11]

4. One guilty of transgressing this commandment is subject to punishment by the courts whether he eats the limb of a living animal or merely the flesh of a living

---

[7] Kitvei Arizal

[8] Babylonian Talmud, Sanhedrin 59a

[9] Mishneh Torah, Laws of Kings, 9:10

[10] Encyclopedia Talmudica, vol.3, p.355

[11] Asarah Ma'amarot, Cheker Din, section 3, chapter 21

animal or any internal organ, even the smallest amount.[12] (The actual transgression has to do only with eating; the use of the animal's hide or any other benefit is permissible.)

5. A person is subject to punishment by the courts for eating the limb or the flesh of either a living domestic or wild animal, but not for eating the limb or flesh of a living chicken.[13] Although the courts do not punish for this, it is forbidden.

Note: Animals, birds, and fish may be killed for food in any way that man deems to be efficient and it should be done as humanely as possible. Slaughtering of animals or birds does not have to be in a ritual manner as with Jews. Fish are considered dead the moment they are taken out of the water, but even so, one may not eat a fish while it appears to be alive, as this is a lack of refinement, and the chief reason for the giving of the Seven Universal Commandments was to refine the nature of man.

---

[12] Mishneh Torah, Laws of Kings, 9:10

[13] Ibid., 9:11. The Ra'avad argues on the Rambam and includes chicken and other fowl.

6. When one slaughters an animal, even if its windpipe and esophagus are severed, so long as the limbs are still moving, the limbs and the meat that are separated from them are forbidden to a Noahide because of this law.[14] However, if one eats the limb or flesh of an animal after it has been killed, but while it is still moving, he is not punished for this by the courts, for it is not actually considered the limb or flesh of a living animal.[15]

7. Whether it is a part of an animal that has meat with sinews, cartilage and bone, such as a leg, or even if it contains no bone material at all, such as the kidneys or the heart or the tongue, it is all the same, that is, it is regarded as a limb for the purposes of this commandment.[16]

8. A limb or piece of flesh that is hanging detached from its original position is not forbidden to be eaten (after the animal is slaughtered) if one could have returned the limb to its original position and the animal could have remained alive for a year. But if one could not have returned this limb to its original position so as to permit

---

[14] Ibid., 9:12

[15] Ibid., 9:11, Radvaz

[16] Chachmat Adam, 27:14

the animal to live for a year, this detached limb is forbidden even after the animal is slaughtered.

9. The foregoing refers only to a limb that is actually hanging, that is, it has been dislodged from its original position and is only slightly attached. However, if a bone were broken in a place that does not cause serious damage to the animal or bird (for example, a wing tip), if flesh covers the majority of the broken limb, then the limb is not forbidden when the animal is slaughtered. If flesh is missing from the major portion of the limb, then the limb has to be removed completely after the animal is slaughtered before the rest of the creature can be eaten.

10. If an animal has an extra limb that is located in its proper area and its presence will not affect the life of the animal, this extra limb is permitted and is not considered like a hanging limb. Double limbs that will affect the life of the animal, such as the stomach, liver, and kidney must be removed, for the law of a hanging limb is applicable to them.

11. Everything that is forbidden to a Jew because of the law of the limb of a living animal is similarly forbidden to a Noahide, except that the latter has the added strictness

of being guilty of this particular transgression whether the animal is spiritually clean or unclean. The Jew is guilty only if the animal is of a type that is spiritually clean.[17]

12. Animals, together with their lives, were given into the hands of mankind. The higher spiritual rank of man dictates that he not eat the limb of a living animal. Even though human flesh and animal flesh are related, the one may be incorporated within the other through eating. But the soul of an animal may never be incorporated within the soul of man. The soul of an animal must first be separated from its physical being before the animal body may be absorbed within and become part of the human body.[18]

13. Vegetarian practices, including those of many religions (even some fundamentalist Christian sects) are generally spurious, and at the very least, reflective of incomplete theology. Lest one think that vegetarianism reflects enlightenment, it is important to remember that

---

[17] Ibid., 27:13

[18] Gen. 9:4, S.R. Hirsch

the ancient Egyptians were religious vegetarians, yet idolaters and moral degenerates in the extreme.[19]

There are four general reasons why a man will likely be a vegetarian. If meat disgusts him, or if he feels that eating meat is unhealthy (particularly in the modern age of pesticides and growth hormones), or if he distrusts the appropriateness of current methods of slaughtering, a person has every right to be a vegetarian. But, if he claims that it is cruel to eat meat, or he is vainly attempting to hearken back to the time of Adam and Eve in the Garden of Eden, he denies the truth of God and places his own understanding of mercy above God's. Since God gave Noah and his descendants the right to eat meat, this right is divine.

A story is told about Rabbi Sholom Ber Schneersohn, who was strolling with his young son, Yosef Yitzchak. As they walked, the young boy idly stretched forth his hand and tore off a leaf from a nearby plant. His father reprimanded him for the act, reminding him that everything in creation has a soul and therefore

---

[19] Yalkut Me'am Loez, Exodus 8:22

one must be careful. If man has need for an object and can take it within the bounds that God has determined, he has a right to it, for man was given dominion over the whole world. But man has no right to wantonly destroy, even to the extent of purposelessly tearing off the leaf of a plant.

Chapter Eleven
The Courts of Law

PART ONE: Roots of the judicial system; jurisdiction of the courts; criteria for judicial decisions; standards within the court system;

Standards and Goals for Judges

1. The Children of Noah are commanded to establish courts of law that will carry out justice and maintain human righteousness and morality in accord with the Seven Universal Commandments.[1] A court system that perverts justice by handing down rulings in conflict with the Seven Universal Laws is an instrument for driving God's blessings out of the world. Anyone who fails to establish a court system, that is, a person who lives in a community or city in which there are no courts, and who does nothing to correct the situation, is punishable by death. One who establishes or maintains courts of law that

---

[1] Mishneh Torah, Laws of Kings, 9:14

operate contrary to the Seven Universal Laws is similarly liable.

In the Book of Genesis (34:25), we learn that two of Jacob's sons, Simeon and Levi, slew every male in the city of Shechem. The prince of the community, Shechem, son of Hamor, had raped their sister, Dinah, and the city failed to execute justice by bringing him to a court of law. The city was therefore guilty of transgressing this seventh of the Seven Universal Laws, and every citizen was liable for punishment.

2. The commandment to establish courts of law, though it might appear to be a positive commandment calling for affirmative action, is considered a prohibition. In effect, the commandment to establish courts of law is a prohibition against failing to establish courts of law, because failure to establish appropriate courts inhibits the performance of justice throughout the nations.[2]

---

[2] Babylonian Talmud, Sanhedrin 59a, Rashi

3. The only punishment meted out by the Noahide courts of law in criminal cases is the death penalty.[3]

4. One accused of a transgression of the Seven Universal Laws and brought to trial in a Noahide court may be convicted only if he is found to be mentally competent.[4]

5. Every individual must accept a legal decision he has received. It is forbidden for an individual to render a judgment himself (vigilante justice) without going to a court of law.[5]

6. In civil matters, that is, cases between individual parties, later authorities question whether the Noahide is commanded to follow the same principles as Jewish law and Jewish courts, or whether he is to follow rulings established by his own Noahide courts and laws.

Although the Noahide courts are responsible for only the Seven Universal Laws, not the 613 commandments of the Torah, there is an opinion that each decision of the Noahide courts must follow its counterpart

---

[3] Ibid. 56b, Rashi

[4] Mishneh Torah, Laws of Kings, 10:2

[5] Encyclopedia Talmudica, vol.3, page 355

in Jewish Law. The accepted opinion, however, is that Noahide judges and courts of law are to render legal decisions according to their own laws and principles of law.

7. In civil matters, arbitration and mediation or any other means of finding an amicable settlement or compromise, thereby avoiding a court trial, is desirable, and, more than that, it is a commandment to seek compromise.

8. Circumstantial evidence is admissible in the Noahide courts of law.

9. The Children of Noah are responsible for knowledge of the Seven Universal Commandments, and therefore one does not have to be warned that he is committing a transgression in order to be accused in a court of law.[6]

10. It is forbidden for a court to have compassion on a murderer, saying that since one person has already been killed, what purpose could there be in killing another?

---

[6] Mishneh Torah, Laws of Kings 9:14

And the court may not delay the execution because of compassion.[7]

11. Similarly, in financial litigation, the court may not have mercy on a poor person, taking the attitude that a rich plaintiff has an obligation to support the poor, therefore finding for the poor defendant so that he will be supported with an honorable livelihood.

12. It is similarly forbidden to pay prejudicial respect to a great person. If two litigants appear in court, one a great wise man and the other a simple person, the judge may not ask about the welfare of the great one nor express pleasure at being in his presence in any way, nor give him honor in any way. Otherwise, the arguments of the simple person would be stifled. He would think, "What's the use anyway?" The judge must not favor either party until judgment is finished. And the sages warn that a judge must not think that since the litigant is so great a person, it is unseemly to embarrass him or see him in his embarrassment.

---

[7] Ibid., Laws of Sanhedrin 20:4

13. If two litigants appear in court, and one is a righteous person while the other is a wicked person, the judge should not presume that the wicked person will not tell the truth, nor presume that he will not change his ways, and therefore the judgment should go against him.[8]

14. One should not judge unrighteously, acquitting the guilty and condemning the innocent. And a judge who delays the judgment, lengthening the time of the testimony or cross-examination, in order to cause either of the litigants to suffer, falls under the ruling of judging unrighteously.[9]

15. One who judges haughtily, without fearing his awesome responsibility and without due deliberation, and then comes to a decision quickly before he has taken the time to carefully consider the case, is considered stupid, wicked, and coarsely egotistical.[10]

16. The courts should not establish a standard judgment by which numerous cases may be judged according to a

---

[8] Ibid., 20:5
[9] Ibid., 20:6
[10] Ibid., 20:7

precedent system, but should consider each case individually on its own unique merits.[11]

(Note: Precedent in legal cases may be followed as guidelines, however.)

17. A case concerning a large sum of money and a case concerning a small amount of money should be given equal and individual consideration.[12]

18. It is a positive commandment to deliver a righteous judgment, treating the two claimants equally in every respect. The judge may not permit one to explain his case at great length while telling the other to keep his words brief. Nor should the judge be pleasant and smile at one while being short and gruff to the other.[13]

19. A judge is forbidden to take a bribe. Bribery will certainly corrupt any judgment. A judge who takes a bribe is obligated to return the bribe if the giver demands it.[14]

---

[11] Ibid., 20:8
[12] Ibid., 20:10
[13] Ibid., 21:1
[14] Ibid., 23:1

20. It is also forbidden to offer a bribe to a judge.[15] The category of bribery is not limited to money, but includes any type of gift or favor.[16]

21. Any judge who sits in judgment and attempts to magnify his importance, even in order to increase the wages of his bailiff or the court clerk, is in the category of one who leans after the wrong things. Once a judge was entering a boat to cross a river. A man who had a case in litigation before the judge was on the boat and stretched out his hand to help the judge aboard. The judge told him, "Behold, I am disqualified to judge your case."

* * *

Note: The goal of justice is to function as impartially and righteously as possible, to the ultimate degree. The following section delineates some of the details of the standards of the Jewish Bet Din, the ecclesiastical court. The Noahide courts are not obligated to follow these rules, but must be acquainted with them as points of reference.

---

[15] Ibid., 23:2

[16] Ibid., 23:3

22. Two litigants appear before a judge. One is dressed very elegantly with expensive clothing and the other is wearing the clothes of a pauper. The judge should tell the elegantly dressed one, "You should clothe the other one until he is dressed as elegantly as you are, or you should clothe yourself to appear as he does, and then you can enter judgment with him."[17]

23. The litigants should both sit or stand; it is improper for one to stand and the other to sit. If the judge wishes to seat them both, he may do so. If they sit, they should sit side by side, neither one higher than the other, and they may so sit during the entire time that the judge is listening to the case. But when the judge's decision is being announced, then both litigants should be standing. The "decision" is the judge's announcement finding for the defendant and against the plaintiff or for the plaintiff and against the defendant. Witnesses for either side should always stand during testimony.[18]

24. If there are many cases before the judge, the case of an orphan should precede the case of a widow, and the

---

[17] Ibid., 21:2

[18] Ibid., 21:3

case of a widow should precede the case of a Torah scholar, and the case of a scholar should precede the case of an unlearned man, and the case of a woman should precede the case of a man, for a woman's embarrassment is greater.[19]

25. It is forbidden for the judge to hear the plea of one of the litigants unless the other one is also present. To listen to even one word of the case itself is forbidden. And we warn the litigant that he should not allow his words to be heard before the other litigant arrives.[20]

26. The judge may not hear testimony through an interpreter or a translator, as the truth is reached only by hearing the words of the litigants themselves. He must understand the language of the litigants and hear their testimony and proofs. If the judge does not speak their language fluently, he may use an interpreter to reply to the litigants to inform them of the judgment and the reason he found for this one and against that one.[21]

---

[19] Ibid., 21:6
[20] Ibid., 21:7
[21] Ibid., 21:8

27. The judge must hear the arguments of the litigants, then review the arguments in their presence to be sure that he understands them clearly. Then he righteously decides the case in his heart, and afterward he reaches the final decision.[22]

28. The judge should not defend the words of the litigant, but he should sit silently as each litigant says what he feels he must. And the judge should not instruct either of the litigants in his presentation of any argument.[23]

29. If the judge sees a favorable point in the case of either of the litigants and the litigant does not know how to bring forth the point, or gets angry and confused to the point of being unable to state his case clearly, the judge may come to his aid slightly and put him on the right track to state the beginning of his case. But the judge must be careful of how he does this so as to avoid instructing the litigant in how to present a meritorious case, for if the judge did this, he would be perverting justice.[24]

---

[22] Ibid., 21:9
[23] Ibid., 21:10
[24] Ibid., 21:11

30. Prior to the judge's hearing the case, if he feels personally threatened by either of the litigants, he may refuse to sit in judgment. But if he has already heard their words and knows which way the judgment is leaning, it is not proper for the judge to refuse to pass judgment out of fear of one of the litigants.[25]

31. If there is more than one judge in a case, it is forbidden for any of them to say after the trial, "I judged in your merit, but my colleagues found against you and inasmuch as they were the majority, what could I do?"[26]

32. A judge is forbidden to sit and judge with a colleague whom he knows to be a thief or a wicked person. He must not sit in judgment with another until he knows with whom he is sitting. And no one should sign a contract until he knows with whom he is signing.[27]

33. A judge is forbidden to judge someone he loves, even though it is less than a great abiding love. Nor can he judge one he hates, even though the person is not his

---

[25] Ibid., 22:1

[26] Ibid., 22:7

[27] Ibid., 22:10

enemy. Ideally, the litigants should be equal in the eyes and heart of the judge. If he recognizes neither them nor their deeds, he can render the most honest judgment possible.[28]

34. Men of learning who are contemptuous of each other should not judge a case together. The judgment is likely to be distorted, as the contempt would incline one to contradict the opinions of the other.[29]

35. A judge should imagine himself with a sword resting on his neck and the Pit of Hell open below him. And he should know Who is the Judge and in front of Whom he judges, and Who will seek retribution from him if he strays from the truth.[30]

36. If a judge feels deeply in his heart that one of the litigants is in the right, and there is no proof for it, or if the judge feels that there is deception and trickery afoot by one of the litigants or with one of the witnesses, and there is no proof for it, or if he feels he cannot rely on the

---

[28] Ibid., 23:6

[29] Ibid., 23:7

[30] Ibid., 23:8

words of the witnesses even if he is not able to disqualify them, or if another similar situation arises, then this judge must disqualify himself from the case and be replaced by one who can judge with a whole heart in the matter. But if the judge knows for sure that one of the witnesses is lying, he should not remove himself from the case, but judge it according to his understanding of the truth. And all these things are matters of the heart.[31]

37. If a judge errs in his decision in a financial matter, he should retract his decision, restore everything to its original status, and retry the case. If it is not possible to retract and restore, for instance, one of the litigants went to a foreign land and took the money awarded him, or the like, then the judge is held harmless from making restitution of the money. It is clear that he had no intention of causing damage.[32]

38. Every judge should possess the following seven attributes:

---

[31] Ibid., 24:1
[32] Ibid., 6:1

Wisdom

Humility

Fear of Heaven

Fear of sin

Contempt for money

Love of truth

Beloved by his fellow man

A good reputation[33]

39. When is one beloved by his fellow man? When he views things in a favorable light and is humble, and he speaks and conducts business in a pleasant manner. He should be meticulous in fulfilling the commandments of God, and he should have conquered his evil inclination to the point that he is without blemish. His name should serve as an outstanding model for the generation. He should be courageous in order to exact a righteous judgment against strong-willed wrongdoers. Money should not be precious to him so that he will not chase after it, for it is taught that if one desires to be rich, poverty will come upon him. He should not need to be exhorted to strive after truth, but should pursue truth from his own

---

[33] Ibid., 2:7

desire for it. He must love truth and despise whatever opposes truth. And he must flee from all forms of transgression.

40. If a judge who possesses all these noble attributes cannot be found, then one should strive to find one who meets as many of these requirements as possible.

PART TWO: Laws concerning witnesses

1. A person may be convicted in a Noahide court by the testimony of a single witness, but only if the witness is known to be righteous.[34] If the character of the witness is not known, it takes two witnesses to be able to convict the accused. It is permissible for the witnesses as well as the judge to be relatives of the accused.[35]

2. A person may testify against himself in a court of law,[36] but since he is the accused, his character is

---

[34] Ibid., Laws of Witnesses, 11:2

[35] Ibid., 9:14

[36] Sefer HaHinnukh, commandment 26

definitely in question, and a second witness is necessary to be able to convict him.

3. The witnesses must be subjected to a thorough and systematic scrutiny to reveal any inconsistencies or other flaws in their testimony.[37]

4. One is commanded to give truthful testimony in a court of law even if he knows the testimony will damage a friend or exonerate an enemy. And, this refers to civil litigation or criminal matters. In a criminal case, he is commanded to come forth and give testimony even if the court does not request him to do so.[38]

5. There are ten classifications that are disqualified as witnesses or as judges in a court of law:

    Women

    Slaves

    Small children

    Fools and the insane

    The deaf and the mute

    The blind, even if they recognize voices

---

[37] Mishneh Torah, Laws of Witnesses, 1:4

[38] Ibid., 1:1

Known transgressors

People who care not how they behave in public

Husbands of women involved in the trial

People who would benefit from a decision in the case[39]

6. A wicked person is disqualified as a witness. This means that the testimony of anyone who is known to transgress the Seven Universal Commandments is inadmissible.[40]

7. The courts should not admit the testimony of anyone unless it is ascertained that this person is involved in keeping the Seven Universal Commandments and does acts of kindness and conducts himself in a straight way and is honest and upright.[41]

8. The judge who admits testimony from a witness before it is ascertained whether the witness is qualified to testify

---

[39] Ibid., 9:1

[40] Ibid., 10:1,2

[41] Ibid., 11:2

is held responsible. This judge is considered as one who perverts justice.[42]

9. Whoever disgraces himself publicly is disqualified as a witness. These are people who walk and eat in a coarse, impolite fashion in public, or who go naked in public, or who are involved in any disgusting work or activity, or anyone who feels no self-embarrassment. All these people are considered on the level of dogs, and one cannot trust them to be stringent against giving false testimony.[43]

10. Even if a multitude of wise, God-fearing people tell someone that they saw such-and-such a person commit such-and-such a crime, and even though he believes it in his heart to be true, he is forbidden to testify in court unless he saw the incident with his own eyes. Anyone who testifies on the hearsay of others is considered a false witness, which is tantamount to conspiring against another, and this is a grave transgression.[44]

---

[42] Ibid., 11:4

[43] Ibid., 11:5

[44] Ibid., 17:1

Note: One who gives false testimony which convicts a person and causes him to be executed receives the death penalty.

Chapter Twelve
Honoring Father and Mother

1. Although the Children of Noah are not commanded to honor father and mother, they have accepted the obligation of performing this meritorious act from the beginning of time and have distinguished themselves through the ages with this righteous behavior.[1]

The Talmud[2] tells the story of Doma ben Nessina, one of the Children of Noah who excelled in the performance of honoring his father to the highest degree. Doma ben Nessina lived in a small village, and it was learned by the Sages of Israel that he had possession of a rare gem that the Sages wanted for the Holy Temple. They traveled to Doma ben Nessina's village and offered him a fabulous sum of money for the gem. He refused their offer because the key to the chest where the gem lay safeguarded was with his father, and his father lay asleep.

---

[1] Nahal Eshkol, Laws of Circumcision, chapter 39, law 11

[2] Babylonian Talmud, Kiddushin 31a

Rather than wake his father, he turned down the Sages' offer, and they returned to Jerusalem.

As a reward for his performance of the commandment of honoring one's father, the next year a red heifer was miraculously born in Doma ben Nessina's herd. (The red heifer, a unique creation that is born only through a miracle, is essential for the performance of one of the ritual purifications in the time of the Holy Temple.) The Sages traveled to Doma ben Nessina again and offered him anything he wanted for his red heifer. Seeing that it was all a miracle from God, he took the same amount they were willing to pay him for the precious gem the year before.

2. One should be extremely meticulous in honoring and respecting one's mother and father, for it is compared to honoring God. Three partners share in the creation of a child: the mother and the father provide the child with a body, and God provides the child with a soul.[3]

---

[3] Kitzur Shulchan Arukh, Chapter 143, Laws 1-22

3. What is considered respecting one's parents? One should not occupy the designated place for one's father in a council of elders, nor should one sit at the designated place of one's parents during meals, nor should one publicly contradict the words of one's parents.

4. What is considered honoring one's parents? One must provide them with food, drink, and clothing from the parents' own funds. If the parents have no funds, the child is obligated to provide for them from his private charity funds. One should escort and help them to and from the house and supply all their needs cheerfully. If a child provides even fattened hens for his parents, but does so rudely, he will receive Divine punishment.

5. If one's mother or father is sleeping and the key to the child's place of business is under their heads, it is forbidden to wake them even if there would be a loss of profit. But, if the parents would benefit from the profit and be saddened by the loss if they were not awakened, it is the child's duty to awaken them and cause them to rejoice over the situation.

If, however, the parent intentionally wanted to cause the son or daughter a financial loss, for example by throwing away money, the child can stop the parent. This is only where the parent has no means of reimbursing the child if the child takes legal recourse. Some say that even if the parent has the means of reimbursement, the child should prevent the parent from causing financial loss in order to avoid the anguish of a legal battle. If the money has already been thrown away, one may not shout at or insult the parent, but may quietly initiate legal proceedings.

6. If the child needs a favor from the community and knows that the favor will be granted because of the esteem in which his parent is held, and if the child also knows that he can obtain the favor based on his own position of esteem, he should not say, "Do it for me because of me," but rather, "Do it for me because of my parent." This way it is an honor for the parent. If, however, the request can be made without personal mention, one does not have to mention the parent.

7. Suppose a mother asks her child to do a task and the child complies, and then, later, the father asks, "Who told you to do this?" If the child feels that by stating, "Mother told me to do it," the father will become angry at the

mother, then the child should incur the father's wrath rather than implicate the mother.

8. Children must rise and remain standing in the presence of their mother or father.

9. One is obligated to honor his mother and father after their deaths. For example, when the child mentions the deceased parent's name, he should add, "May his (or her) memory be blessed in the World to Come," or, "May he (or she) rest in peace."

10. Even if the father or mother are wicked and transgress the Seven Commandments, the child must honor and revere them. Even a child born to a forbidden union is obligated to honor and revere his parents. Others hold that one does not have to honor and revere wicked parents until they repent of their deeds, but it is forbidden to cause them grief. However, it is better to follow the first opinion.

11. If a child sees a parent transgress one of the Seven Commandments, the child should not chastise the parent in a rude way by saying, "You have violated one of the commandments." Rather, the child should put it in the

form of a question, such as, "Father (or Mother), doesn't it state in the Seven Laws of Noah such-and-such?" In this manner, the correction comes in the way of the child seeking information rather than reprimanding. The parent will understand the implication, correct himself or herself, and will not be embarrassed.

12. If the parents tell the child to transgress one or more of the Seven Noahide Laws, the child should not listen. The parents have an obligation to honor God, and therefore the child has to honor God's wishes before the wishes of the parent.

13. Both men and women have an obligation to honor and revere their parents. However, a married woman owes her devotion to her husband and is exempt from honoring her mother and father. But if he does not object, she is obliged to honor her parents as much as possible.

14. Whoever shames his or her mother or father, even with words or gestures, is considered cursed by God, as it says, "Cursed is the one who dishonors his father or mother" (Deut. 27:16).

15. If the mother or father have a splinter deeply imbedded, the son or daughter may not remove it because a wound may result, and a child is forbidden to inflict any kind of a wound on a parent. Even if the child is a doctor, he may not operate, though his intention may be only to heal. However, this is only in the case where there are other doctors available. Where the need is pressing and only the child can help, he or she may do whatever is necessary.

16. If one's parents have become mentally ill, God forbid, the child should attempt to act with them in accord with their mental state until God will have mercy on them. If the situation becomes aggravated and the child can no longer handle it, then he or she must leave the parents in the charge of professionals.

17. A parent should not be too exacting in demanding honor from the child, but be forgiving and overlook the shortcomings of a child.

18. A parent should not strike a grown child. This refers to the child's maturity, not his chronological age, and is based on the specific nature of the child. If a parent sees that a grown child has a rebellious nature, he should

reason and discuss the situation with the child. Striking the child will only aggravate matters.

19. A child is obligated to honor a stepmother as long as the father is still living. Also the child must honor a stepfather so long as the mother is still living. It is also proper conduct to honor the stepmother or stepfather even after the death of one's own parent.

20. One must honor an older brother even if he is only a half brother.

21. A man must honor his father-in-law and mother-in-law as one would honor any other important elder, through kind words and good deeds.

22. One who truly wishes to honor his mother and father should study and observe the Seven Laws of the Children of Noah and should perform good deeds. It is the greatest honor possible for the parents when people say, "Happy are the parents who raised such a child."

But a child who does not walk in the right path brings reproach to the parents and disgraces them in the most severe way. Furthermore, parents who are concerned about the welfare of their children should be involved in the learning and practice of the Seven Laws of the Children of Noah and should perform acts of kindness so that they may please God and their fellow man and make their children proud of them. One who does not do so disgraces the children. And worse than this, children suffer for the sins of their parents, as it says, "Visiting the transgression of the fathers upon the children unto the third and fourth generation of them that hate Me" (Exod. 20:5).

There is no cruelty greater than causing the death of one's own child through one's sins. Conversely, no one exhibits more compassion for his children than a righteous person, as it says, "And showing mercy unto the thousandth generation of them that love Me" (Exodus 20:6).

Chapter Thirteen
Charity

1. There was a pious man who was quite charitable, helping all those in need. Once, he set out in a boat and a storm came and sank his boat in the sea. Rabbi Akiva witnessed the event and went to report the tragic news, but before he could tell anyone, he looked up and there was the man standing before him.

"Aren't you the one who went down in the sea?" Rabbi Akiva asked him.

"Yes, I am the same," he replied.

"And who raised you out of the sea?" Rabbi Akiva asked.

"The charity I practiced raised me out of the sea," the man said.

"How do you know this?" Rabbi Akiva asked him.

The man told him, "When I sank to the depths, I heard the great roar of the waves of the sea, one wave calling to another, 'Hurry, let us raise this man out of the sea for he practices charity every day of his life.'"

Rabbi Akiva smiled and declared, "Blessed be God, the God of Israel, Who has chosen the words of the Torah and the words of the Sages, and established them forever and to all eternity, for it is written, "ast your bread upon the waters, and you shall find it after many days (Ecclesiastes 11:1)," and 'Charity rescues from death'" (Proverbs 10:2).[1]

2. It is a positive commandment to give charity,[2] as it says, "The life of your brother is with you" (Lev. 25:36). Anyone who sees a poor person requesting funds and purposely ignores this person and does not give him charity has transgressed, as it says, "You should not harden your heart, nor should you close your hand from your poor brother" (Deut. 15:7).

---

[1] Avot of Rabbi Nathan

[2] Kitzur Shulchan Arukh, Chapter 31:1-16

3. It is a general principle that a person does not become poor by giving charity. Nor does an evil or destructive thing occur through one's giving charity. Also, if one has mercy on others, the One Above has mercy on him.

4. One is forbidden to tempt God, that is, to perform any action on the condition that God reveal His Presence. The single exception to this is the act of giving charity. The Torah promises that God will repay anyone who gives charity and a person is bidden to give in order to test God.

5. God is close to poverty-stricken people, as it says, "And the cry of the poor will He hear" (Job 34:28). Therefore, one has to be careful about the supplications of poor people.

6. Every person has the obligation to give charity according to his ability. Even a poor person who supports himself from charity may give charity from these funds. Though he can afford only a little, this should not prevent him from giving charity. A little charity from a poor man is considered as worthy as a great amount given by a rich person. As the Sages say, "When one offers a sacrifice, it does not matter if the offering is an ox or a bird or flour, whether it is a large offering or a small offering, the main

criterion is that the giver directs his heart to his Father in Heaven."[3] But if one has only enough for his sustenance, he has no obligation to give charity. A person has a priority of providing for himself before he provides for others.

7. The community should supply every need that a poor person lacks. The people of the city are obligated to supply him whatever he is lacking to maintain the level he was accustomed to before he became poor, and they should give it to him discreetly, so that few know he is receiving it.

8. If a poor person is collecting from door to door publicly, one should give him a small donation according to the poor man's situation.

9. The community should provide each poor person with at least the equivalent of two meals a day and a place to sleep.

10. A person should give charity in the following manner: the first year of his going into business, he should donate

---

[3] Babylonian Talmud, Menahot 110a

at least ten percent of his capital. After that he should give ten percent of the profits earned from his capital after first deducting his expenses. This is the average way to give charity. Most respectable to give is twenty percent of the principle the first year, and in succeeding years twenty percent after annual profits. One who is not self-employed but earns his money on a salary basis should give the ten to twenty percent based on his net income after taxes.

11. One who wants to conduct himself in an honorable way should conquer his evil inclination and widen his hand. Anything that is done for the glory of God should be done gracefully. If he feeds a starving person, he should feed him with the finest foods that he can offer. When he clothes someone who is threadbare, he should clothe him in the finest apparel he can offer.

12. Gifts given to one's parents, who need to be supported through charity, are considered charity. Furthermore, they take precedence over others.

13. Charity to relatives takes precedence over charity to strangers. The poor living in one's own house take precedence over the poor living in one's city. The poor of one's city take precedence over the poor of another city,

as it says in the verse, "to your brother, to your poor and to your needy" (Deut. 15:11). However, one whose responsibility is the distribution of communal funds for charity (not just his own contributions alone), should be careful that he does not give more to his needy relatives than to other people.

14. If anyone gives charity to a poor person, and gives it with a sour countenance and a feeling of condescension, even if he gives gold pieces, he has lost all the merit of his actions. This person has transgressed the verse, "And your heart shall not grieve when you give to him" (Deut. 15:10). One must give with a sense of joy and a cheerful countenance, and he should console the poor person on his tribulations, cheering him with words of comfort.

15. It is forbidden to reject the requests of a poor person and turn him away empty-handed even if all one can afford at the time is a morsel of food. If there is really nothing in one's hand to give, then one should say kind words to the person indicating that he sincerely wishes to give him something, but that it is not possible at this time. (And it is better not to give at all if all one has is a small

coin and it is known for certain that giving a small coin will grieve or offend the poor person.)

16. It is forbidden to rebuke or to raise your voice to the poor, as their hearts are broken and humbled. Woe to one who disgraces a poor person. Rather one should be like a parent to the poor, demonstrating mercy in deed and word.

17. If one should say, "I am obligating myself to give such-and-such amount to charity," or, "I am giving this specific bill of currency to charity," that person is obligated to give the money he has pledged immediately or as soon as possible. It is considered a transgression to delay if one has the ability to honor the obligation. If there are no poor people to whom to give the money, it should be set aside until a poor person is found.

18. If a person says, "I will give such an amount of money to this specific person," he can wait until the person comes to him. He does not have to seek him out.

19. Anyone is permitted to set aside money for charity to distribute according to whatever manner and to whomever he sees fit.

19. One who convinces others to give charity earns greater reward than one who actually gives.

20. If one distributes money to the poor and the poor in turn insult him, he should not be concerned, as his merit is now far greater because of the humiliation he has borne.

21. The highest level of giving charity is to assist a person financially before he becomes poor, thus preventing him from becoming poor. Such assistance should be given graciously in the form of a gift or a loan or an offering of partnership in a financial venture or a job placement so that the poor person will not be forced to seek financial assistance from others.

22. One should attempt, if at all possible, to give charity secretly. The best way of giving charity is when the giver does not know to whom the money is going and the receiver does not know from whom it came.

23. One should not boast about one's personal acts of charity; self-glorification causes the merit that has been attained to be lost. But if one donated any object for charity, he may inscribe his name on it so that it will serve

as a memorial. Also, one may publicize his acts of charity if the public knowledge will inspire others to give.

24. A person should try to avoid becoming the recipient of charity. Even suffering a certain degree of hardship is preferable to becoming dependent on another person. It is, however, improper to subject others to hardship, such as one's wife and child, because of an unwillingness to take charity.

25. Anyone who does not need charity, but through deceit obtains such funds will come to be dependent on other people. Conversely, one who truly needs charity to the extent that he cannot really live without such funds, such as an old person without an income, or a sick person, or one with a large family to support and daughters whose marriages he must pay for, if he refuses to accept charity out of pride, he is considered like one who spills blood and will be held responsible for his actions. All he will have to show for his suffering are sins. However, one who needs charity, but chooses to suffer deprivation, not because of pride, but because he does not want to become a public burden, will not die before he has risen to support other poor people.

26. It says in the Midrash Rabba,[4] "A door which does not open for the poor will surely open for the physician."

---

[4] Midrash Rabba, Song of Songs, Chapter 6, Section 17

Chapter Fourteen
Sacrifices

1. The reason man lacks a sensitivity to and understanding of animal sacrifices dates back to a period of time just before the building of the Second Temple. It was a time when idolatry was rampant. Man was said to truly lust after idol worship. The situation was so desperate that the Sages of Israel prayed to God to remove man's deep yearning for idolatry. When the prayers were accepted, a lion of fire was seen to burst forth from the curtain of the Holy of Holies. The Sages understood God's answer. Since He had created the world in such a way that good and evil are always balanced to afford man free choice, when the desire for idolatry was removed, the balance was maintained by removing man's understanding of sacrifices.[1]

In brief, offering an animal sacrifice symbolized the subjugation and destruction of man's animal nature. The animal was slaughtered then burned on the altar,

---
[1] Babylonian Talmud, Yoma 69b

reducing it to its elements which ascended on high. By meditating on this process, a person was able to nullify his animal self, thus bringing him closer to God. And we find that the Hebrew word for sacrifice is *korban* which comes from the root *karav,* meaning close, since the *korban* brought man close to God.[2]

Since the time of the destruction of the Holy Temple, the Jews were promised that study of the laws of sacrifices and prayer would be acceptable to God in lieu of the actual sacrifices, as it is written, "We will render the prayer of our lips in place of the sacrifice of bullocks" (Hos. 14:3).

What about the Children of Noah? In the times of the Holy Temple, the righteous among them who followed the Seven Universal Laws were permitted to dwell in the Land of Israel and to enter the Temple and to offer sacrifices to God. Moreover, sacrifices were offered on behalf of the nations of the world by the Jewish priests,

---

[2] Jerusalem, Eye of the Universe, Aryeh Kaplan, Chapter 5

most notably the seventy bullocks offered during the holiday of Sukkot, the Festival of Booths.[3]

If, after the destruction of the Holy Temple, the Jew could offer his sacrifices to God in a spiritual way by prayer and study, what could the Noahide do?

The answer is a great surprise. Although the Jew is forbidden to offer sacrifices anywhere but in the Holy Temple, the Noahide, in the opinion of many authorities, is permitted to build private altars and present offerings to the God of Israel upon them even today![4] (This in no way implies that a Noahide is discouraged from praying to God.)

Although the laws of sacrifices are complex indeed and outside the scope of this volume, the following points are a brief digest of their general principles.

---

[3] Babylonian Talmud, Sukkah 55b

[4] Ibid., Zevachim 116b, Mishneh Torah, Laws of Sacrifices, 19:16

2. During the times when the Holy Temple stood in Jerusalem, a Noahide was permitted to bring a *korban olah,* a burnt offering wholly consumed by fire.[5]

3. The Noahide is permitted to bring spiritually clean wild animals, such as members of the deer family, as well as spiritually clean domestic animals. Spiritually clean animals are those that have split hooves and chew their cud. He may also bring spiritually clean birds, even roosters. Chickens and spiritually clean wild animals are permissible only when the Noahide is offering them on his private altar.[6] When he brings an offering to God in the Holy Temple, it must correspond to those kinds prescribed by the Torah and Jewish Law.

4. The offering of a Noahide must have all its limbs to be valid. Other blemishes and minor disfigurements do not render the offering invalid. This leniency is applicable only when the sacrifice is offered on one's own private altar. When the Children of Noah bring sacrifices to the

---

[5] Ibid., 3:3

[6] Babylonian Talmud, Zevachim 115b

Holy Temple, they are acceptable only if they meet the criteria of a Jewish offering.[7]

5. The Children of Noah may construct altars and offer their sacrificial offerings in any location.

6. One may only offer a *korban olah,* the burnt offering, which demonstrates a desire to cling to the God of Israel. This offering is entirely consumed by fire and is among the most holy of the sacrifices. It is slaughtered on the north side of the altar, and its blood is received in a service vessel at the north side of the altar. Its blood is then dashed against the northeast corner and the southwest corner of the altar, thereby spreading out along all four walls. These sacrifices require that the hides of the animals be given to the *kohanim* (Jewish priests). The flesh of the animal is then to be flayed and cut in pieces before it is entirely consumed by the altar's fire.[8]

7. Since most authorities today forbid *kohanim* from accepting their portion of the sacrificial offerings, doubt

---

[7] Encyclopedia Talmudica, Sons of Noah, vol.3, p.357

[8] Mishneh Torah, Laws of Sacrifices, 6:1-23

exists regarding the permissibility of these sacrifices from the Children of Noah.

8. One who knowingly offers an invalid sacrifice is liable for punishment.

9. Some authorities contend that if a Noahide offers a sacrifice that is missing a limb, he transgresses a positive commandment, but it is not a transgression of one of the Seven Laws of the Children of Noah, which would require punishment in a court of law.[9] Others say that there is no transgression at all, but the sacrifice is merely rendered invalid.[10]

---

[9] Babylonian Talmud, Avodah Zarah 5b; Tosefos, "From where do we know…"

[10] Ritvah on Tosefos, footnote 7

Chapter Fifteen
Prayer

The following is a free translation from the responsa of Rabbi Moshe Feinstein, of blessed memory, concerning the matter of prayer and the Noahide:[1]

When a Noahide prays he certainly obtains reward as we learn from the Prophet Isaiah, "My abode shall be declared a house of prayer unto all the nations of the world" (Isa. 56:7).

Even though they are not commanded to engage in prayer, it is evident that a Noahide does fulfill a commandment whenever he prays.

Note: In the preface, it was stated that commandment is a translation of the Hebrew word, mitzvah, which also means connection with God.

When a Noahide is pressed by personal emergency, he is definitely expected to pray to God. Such

---

[1] Iggerot Moshe, Orach Chaim, vol.2, responsum 25, pp. 196-198

prayer demonstrates a basic belief in God, exhibiting trust that He alone gives sustenance and that He alone heals. One who does not pray to God in time of dire need demonstrates that he does not believe in Him but in other forces.

The question arises, if a Noahide prays merely in his thoughts will he merit reward or must he pray verbally? We must conclude that he would not be rewarded for mental prayer as it is not prayer performed in the proper manner. Since prayer is a bond between the physical being and a personal God, one must use physicality to create this bond, which means verbal prayer.

The Noahide's prayer should not consist solely of supplications but should also include praises to God.

The act and experience of praying to God (and it should be obvious that it is forbidden to pray to any being other than God) has limitless levels. Whether one supplicates God for his needs and wants, or for help in times of danger or stress, or engages in deep meditational prayer in order to elevate oneself spiritually, prayer is always a mystical experience, a communion with the infinite Creator of one's own soul. Through prayer, man can strip his consciousness from all materialism and physicality, divorcing himself from his animal nature, and become a totally spiritual being. Through prayer, one can attain a level close to that of prophecy.[2]

And King David wrote, "Praise the Lord, all nations, extol Him all the peoples" (Ps. 117:1). This verse from Psalms refers specifically to the prayers of the Children of Noah.

* * * *

"And the dove came to him at the time of evening and, behold, an olive leaf plucked in her mouth, so Noah knew that the waters had abated from upon the face of the earth. And he waited yet another seven days, and he sent forth the dove and she did not continue to return to him again" (Gen. 8:10-12).

This dove with the olive branch in her beak is the universal symbol of peace. The Talmud teaches that the dove said, "Rather my food be bitter as the olive branch

---

[2] Jerusalem, Eye of the Universe, Aryeh Kaplan, Chapter 5

in the hand of the Holy One, blessed be He, than sweet as honey in the hand of flesh and blood" (*Eruvin* 18).

"Behold I will send you Elijah the Prophet before the coming of the great and awesome day of the Lord. And he will turn the heart of the fathers to the children and the heart of the children to the fathers" (Malachi 3:23,24).

Printed in Great Britain
by Amazon